Zero's Neighbour

Zero's Neighbour

SAM BECKETT

Hélène Cixous

Translated with additional notes by Laurent Milesi

polity

First published in French as *Le Voisin de zéro* © Éditions Galilée, 2007

This book is supported by the French Ministry of Foreign Affairs, as part of the Burgess programme run by the Cultural Department of the French Embassy in London (www.frenchbooknews.com)

This English edition © Polity Press, 2010

Polity Press
65 Bridge Street
Cambridge CB2 1UR, UK

Polity Press
350 Main Street
Malden, MA 02148, USA

ISBN-13: 978-0-7456-4415-8
ISBN-13: 978-0-7456-4416-5(pb)

A catalogue record for this book is available from the British Library.

Typeset in 11 on 15 pt Adobe Garamond
by Servis Filmsetting Ltd, Stockport, Cheshire
Printed and bound by MPG Books Group, UK

The publisher has used its best endeavours to ensure that the URLs for external websites referred to in this book are correct and active at the time of going to press. However, the publisher has no responsibility for the websites and can make no guarantee that a site will remain live or that the content is or will remain appropriate.

Every effort has been made to trace all copyright holders, but if any have been inadvertently overlooked the publisher will be pleased to include any necessary credits in any subsequent reprint or edition.

For further information on Polity, visit our website: www.politybooks.com

Contents

How can one translate a text written 'in two tongues in French' (p. 39) that is 'written through' another writer who translated-rewrote himself back and forth across two languages till the exhaustion of his minimalist tongue 'in the vicinity of zero'? Or, as Jacques Derrida might have said, how can one experience the impossible in translation as the crossing of a desert when one needs to retreat into what intractably resists in and across idioms?[1] Such is the 'task' facing the translator of *Le Voisin de zéro*, who, as he toils along, discovers that he must adaptively cast aside all systems, theories and rules, and learn when not to translate 'from French into English', as he is conventionally expected to, but rather to translate French *into* English performatively, the *français* having to become *English* whenever a more ethically literal[2] translation would go against the original's insistence on its own linguistic act. Thus, to practise what can be called an *in-traduction*, tra-ducting – in both its now obsolete senses of transferring/transporting and translating – within a 'foreign' language while re-marking the original in its address. Such a structural permutation is at work in the following sequence, rendered 'back to front' (i.e. swapping source and target languages) – rather than attempting to resort to an equivalent of French *verlan* words in back slang – in order to adhere to the performative dimension of the original passage, which parades the untranslatability of its idiom:

> *Ouf.* Par exemple. (Ça c'est intraduisible, n'est-ce pas? Faire ouf, Être <u>ne peut le faire qu'en français</u>. Pareil pour faire Œuf, ou faire Feu. Mais dans chaque langue on se débrouillera pour faire ouf autrement.) <u>Rien qu'en français</u>. Nous notons: faire ouf! ou bien faire *ououf*! ouf [. . .]. <u>*Whew!*</u>[3]

> <u>*Whew*</u>. For example. (That's untranslatable, isn't it? To whew. <u>Who can do so only in English</u>. Same for to whoa, or to whoosh. But in each language one will wangle a way to whew otherwise.) <u>Just in English</u>. We note: to whew! or *phew*! whew [. . .]. <u>*Ouf!*</u>
> (p. 33)

But what happens when Cixous's text re-marks (on) its linguistic medium and act of enunciation in a context emphasizing Beckett's adoption of, and fidelity to, the same French language? Double-bind with a twist: one cannot 'translate into English' without betraying Beckett's linguistic allegiance in an alien speech act, nor can one still manage to express oneself in French like the original, which can confidently state *'puisque je m'adresse à vous en français'*. . . Unless one takes the Cixousian performance at its own word (*'ce qui n'empêche pas de passer d'un bord à l'autre de E à F et de F à E'*) and translates 'in effect', plying back and forth between the two edges by playing on the double (Anglo-Saxon, Romance) vein of the English language and even introducing a touch of Gallicism as a make-believe. *Traduttore, traditore*: the age-old cliché of the *belles infidèles* is here given a renewed lease of life in this paradoxical problematic of how one needs to betray in order to be faithful. The following excerpt occurs soon after a dense idiomatic weaving of *dis, faire* and *diffère*, for which an equivalent could have been found in English (e.g. be, come, become; gain, say, gainsay) but to radically 'different' effects, hence the decision to foreground the French puns within the English. The interlingual translation is held together by the initial *intraduction* of 'fare' (p. 41), by being deliberately unfaithful to infidelity itself as *'infidèle'* becomes 'unfair', by the insertion of 'in spite of appearances' to introduce the un-French 'I am addressing myself to you in French', and, further in the text, in the rendering of *'tout compte fait'* as 'when all is said and done':

> En faisant cette chose devant vous en français je ne suis tout de même pas infidèle à Beckett, pas plus pas

moins que lui. [. . .] mais cette conférence [. . .] est au secret ici, en réserve, et répandue partout sous chaque page et dans chaque phrase, puisque <u>je m'adresse à vous en français</u>, langue élue de Beckett, apres peu d'hésitations, ce qui n'empêche pas de passer d'un bord à l'autre de E à F et de F à E, c'est selon [. . .].[4]

<u>As I am doing all this in French in front of you</u>, I am still <u>not being unfair to Beckett</u>, not more not less than him. [. . .] but this lecture [. . .] is in secret here, in reserve, and spread everywhere beneath each page and in each sentence, since <u>in spite of appearances I am addressing myself to you in French</u>, the language elected by Beckett after few hesitations, which does not prevent one from stepping or passing from one edge to the other from E to F and from F to E, depending on the setup [. . .]. (pp. 41–2)

Le français must know when and when not to become *English* to secure the *eff*ect and ben*ef(f)*it (see p. 42) of a translation which also has to negotiate and convey a movement of *trans-lation*, the impossible 'inter(-) diction' of a trans-linguistic experiment or passage. A dissymmetrical symmetry, E F F E (English French– French English), for instance that of the translation in effect of '*efflanquée*' as 'effete' within a self-consciously *eff*able sequence:

Rien qu'à voir les deux volumes faux jumeaux du Harrap's Dictionary ou un autre, c'en est fait pour Sam et son appétit pour le maigre, rien qu'à poser côte à côte le mince F.E. alors qu'à côté E.F. est deux fois plus gros gras lourd lard proliférant volumineux, naturellement, et pour ainsi dire, congénitalement, Beckett est du parti de l'efflanqué [. . .].[5]

Just take a look at the two false twin volumes of *Harrap's Dictionary* or another and Sam's appetite for the lean is effectively done for, just put side by side the thin F.E. whereas in comparison E.F. is twice as big fat thick heavy proliferating voluminous, naturally, and so to speak, congenitally, Beckett, poor him, has been on the side of the effete [. . .]. (pp. 42–3)

Cixous's 'numerical' study[6] of Beckett can be read indirectly as an ad-hoc translation manual, complete with (stage) directions for use in order to zero in on the right choice between literality, literarity and all forms of (trans-linguistic) adaptation, 'not more not less':

While approaching the exact thing, thus first approximation and error, in order to correct the error you estimate the error by committing a smaller error, you approach the exact thing, the end, by making finer and finer errors. Variant: the alternate series. It's

less great, it's less small or it's too great it's too small,
correct, every other term by default, every other term
by negative excess [. . .], there's a little lacking, there's
a little too much, again, correct, approach [. . .].
(p. 48)

This sort of constant adjustment has also regulated
our approach to rendering Cixous's deceptively semi-
citational prose, and some of the unexpected discrepan-
cies between the French text and this English translation
can be traced back to the gap between her working
through Beckett's French and, consequently, the neces-
sity for us to translate through, or at the very least take
into account, Beckett's English. This gap has been partially 'corrected' whenever her own commentary relays
French quotations and thus requires closer proximity to
the linguistic material she is working from, regardless of
Beckett's own English adaptations. As much as possible
where it was felt to be necessary, though without wishing
to be exhaustive in the light of such a near-constant practice, sources in the Beckett corpus have been supplied in
endnotes.

Laurent Milesi

1 See Jacques Derrida, *Monolingualism of the Other; or, The Prosthesis of Origin*, trans. Patrick Mensah (Stanford: Stanford University Press, 1998), p. 72.

2 See, for example, Antoine Berman, *La Traduction et la lettre, ou l'auberge du lointain* (Paris: Seuil, 1999) and Lawrence Venuti, 'Strategies of Translation', *The Routledge Encyclopedia of Translation Studies*, ed. Mona Baker (London and New York: Routledge, 1998), pp. 240–4.

3 Hélène Cixous, *Le Voisin de zéro. Sam Beckett* (Paris: Galilée, 2007), pp. 45-46. Throughout this introduction elements we wish to highlight for specific attention in quotations and in the translation have been underlined and the French interpolations within square brackets in the translation have been omitted.

4 Cixous, *Le Voisin de zéro*, p. 55.

5 Cixous, *Le Voisin de zéro*, p. 56.

6 For the relation between algebra and translation, see Laurent Milesi, 'Algébrie à l'irlandaise: *Le Voisin de zéro*', in *Cixous sous X, d'un coup le nom*, ed. Marie-Dominique Garnier and Joana Masó (Saint-Denis: Presses de l'Université de Vincennes, 2010), pp. 149–58.

Why, Beckett, I can love him, a rare, precious *can*, I who am not on the side of grey blackness, I can love him, *frozen and collapsing endlessly*, I who'd rather leap, cross all the thick, opaque, *slothful*, luxuriously *slothful* zones of his fog, in order to come and love him all the same, thus like my next of kin? Because of his insistence on being himself from yesterday to the beyond, from today onwards, himself faithful to himself, on being inflexibly the very selfsame, no matter how broken or broken in, without adulteration, on always having been the one he would be and conversely on endlessly becoming the one he would always already have been incorruptibly, the being before the end, all life long and all the time of times forever *owing before the end* [devant la fin]. He owes the end, owes it to himself, owes it to us, all his life crept [*rampée*] owing before the end, without death, spent vamping [*vamper*] the end, in vain, camping [*camper*] *in the vicinity of zero*. Dreaming of zero, because of the cawing-wailing-rattle of his Belacquian voice, because he will have gone round the purgatorial world purging as much as purged, lame-limping along to come back reduced to almost nothing, the same on the same time-worn soles.

It was on 14 August 1922. Proust was going. 'And if the world were coming to an end, what would you do?' the newspaper *L'Intransigeant* had asked – a little question. To come to an end. How wonderful life would suddenly appear to us, said the one who was going. Then our *laziness*, which ceaselessly postpones life, would be undone. If the world were coming to an end, in the end, I would live, the dying man said, I would wrench myself free from *negligence*.

It was on 9 December 1989. Beckett was going. 'I'm done', he said. And now that the world is coming to an end, V., a curious voice, will ask Beckett, what will you say? 'Was there much of the journey you found worthwhile?' Answer: 'Precious little.' Two words. Untranslatable. *Qu'est-ce que ça valait, ce voyage? Bien peu. Pas grand-chose* (Not much). Precious little. Literally in French: *précieusement peu*. A fine idiomatic oxymoron. What is precious is little, precious little. I can love such a little.

Precious little. For Proust the five visitations: cobble spoon plate napkin water-pipe, cup. The keys of his life-works. For his successor: skull, stick, sand, sky, grey, ray in the dark. The Almost-Nothings of the whole that make up the Whole.

Cruel Sam Beckett, yes, no, of a disaffected, natural,

structural, white cruelty, a white cruelty, perhaps grey but less and less, still less and less, more still, faithfully cruel without blood, without a drop of blood, that would be too crude, no, self-cruelty, not without a compassion, white or grey, but without any piety, a compassion accompanying the character, indistinct but similar, if not of solidarity, no, but at least of an echo, of a – co. A small minimum of *with*. There, in the minimal, most infinite company remains that which will have never abandoned Beckett, will have never been abandoned, writing, or the text. No matter how rasped, clipped, denied, the tone and the rotunda managed to have been, he will have always, regularly, *sam*ilarly signed Sam. As early as the first words, these are already, similarly, the last words. I admire that. As early as the first flight of the artist Trinity College–ENS Ulm a single without return. He has read, seen, known, thrown it all Dublin, Joyce, Florence, Paris, you bet, Dante, Mandelstam, nothing has encroached upon him, nor anybody upon his rock, he remains the same giant hunched up on a pebble. Like the other giant, his only next of kin, Proust, whom he paints leaning over *this shallow well of an inscrutable banality: a cup*. Proust a giant and his cup of the world, the only giant and cup he can swallow, Proust is, because Joyce sticks in his throat. Proust's genius, he will have gobbled it up. He is twenty-four years old. Proust has just died. I should have said fallen. Straightaway Beckett picks him up, the giant and his uneven cobble. Beckett's *echo's bones* version of Proust.

Hélène Cixous

Without Tom Bishop's confident commission I would not have had the courage to overcome my laziness to Beckett the immense Beckett. It is thanks to Tom and his fault, *felix culpa*, and out of fidelity to the enthusiastic fidelity of this eternal Beckettian that I have attempted to scale the ante-purgatorial rotunda.

Tomorrow, and tomorrow, and tomorrow
Creeps in this petty pace from day to day
To the last syllable of recorded time,

And all our yesterdays have lighted fools
The way to dusty death. Out, out, brief candle!
Life's but a walking shadow, a poor player
That struts and frets his hour upon the stage,
And then is heard no more. It is a tale
Told by an idiot, full of sound and fury,
Signifying nothing.

William Shakespeare, *Macbeth*, Act V, sc. v, ll.
19–28

Given how long he's been letting out Beckett's cry at every other step: 'out, out, brief candle',[1] for a hundred years and more, this brevity, this precocious old age, in the hundred years he's been creeping 'in this petty pace' from day to day softly – dying [*mou – rir*] feeling all the time passing to approach 'the last syllable of recorded time'. One soft – long pause – *laugh* dying out [*mou – un long temps* – rire], last syllable,

why, Beckett, I can love him, a rare, precious *can*,[2] I who am not on the side of grey blackness, I can love him, *frozen and collapsing endlessly*,[3] I who'd rather leap, cross all the thick, opaque, *slothful*, luxuriously *slothful* zones of his fog, in order to come to love him all the same, thus like my next of kin? Because of his insistence on being himself from yesterday to the beyond, from today onwards, himself faithful to himself, on being inflexibly the very selfsame, no matter how broken or broken in, without adulteration, on always having been the one he would be and conversely on endlessly becoming the one he would always already have been incorruptibly, because of the cawing-wailing-rattle of his Belacquian[4]

1

voice, because he will have gone round the purgatorial world purging as much as purged, lame-limping along[5] to come back reduced to almost nothing, the same on the same time-worn soles, because he has always been never ceasing to be the same[6] Sam before Shem Sham Shaun Joyce,[7] during and after Joyce because, before signing as masked Belacqua, he has already unmasked in himself Dante. . . Proust. . . Vico. . . Joyce,[8] because he has never lied deceived resembled, only oscillated before being as he must [*devant être*], so much Sam, and maybe – *sam*, *Grausam*[9] should I say in honour of his genius for the German language, Sam (Sam I'll come back to it in two lines) – so *grau* – *gris* grey self-Sam, that it seems he never donned the hat of Samuel his biblical predecessor, too long Samuel, I come back to shorter-Sam, *am*. *Grau-sam*, a word, two words, more than/no more of one language[10] to name the affect which has been beating in the whole of his mental rotunda[11] from the first to the last sigh, pause. *Temps. Un temps.* He was, is *grausam*, then, a little like everybody, and absolutely like nobody, *Grau-sam*, *Gris-Sam*, Grey-Sam – but first I borrow Freud's German word in order to synonymize the human: that is to say, *Cruel.*[12]

Cruel Sam Beckett, yes, no, of a disaffected, natural, structural, white cruelty, a white, perhaps grey cruelty but less and less, still less and less, more still, faithfully cruel without blood [*sans sang*], without a drop of blood,[13] that would be too crude, no, self-cruelty, not without a compassion, white or grey, but without any piety, a compassion accompanying the character, indistinct but similar, if not one of solidarity, no, but at least of an echo, of a – co. A small minimum of *with*. There, in the minimal, most infinite company remains that which will have never abandoned Beckett, will have never been abandoned, writing, or the text. No matter how rasped, clipped, denied, the tone and the rotunda managed to have been, he will have always, regularly, *sam*ilarly signed Sam. As early as the first words, they are already, similarly, the last words. I admire that. As early as the first flight of the artist Trinity College–ENS Ulm a single without return. He has read, seen, known [*su*], thrown [*chu*] it all Dublin, Joyce, Florence, Paris, you bet,[14] Dante, Mandelstam, nothing has encroached upon him, nor anybody upon his rock [*caillou*], he remains the same giant hunched up on a pebble.[15] Like the other giant, his only next of kin, Proust, whom he paints leaning over *this shallow well of an inscrutable banality: a cup*.[16] Proust a giant and his cup of the world, the only giant and cup he can swallow, Proust is, because Joyce sticks in his throat. Proust's genius, he will have gobbled it up. He is twenty-four years old. Proust has just died. I should have said fallen. Straightaway Beckett picks him up, the giant and his uneven cobble.[17] Beckett's *echo's bones*[18] version of Proust.

It was on 14 August 1922. Proust was going. 'And if the world were coming to an end, what would you do?'

3

the newspaper *L'Intransigeant* had asked – a little question. To come to an end. How wonderful life would suddenly appear to us, said the one who was going. Then our *laziness*, which ceaselessly postpones life, would be undone.[19] If the world were coming to an end, in the end, I would live, the dying man said, I would wrench myself free from *negligence*.

It was on 9 December 1989. Beckett was going. 'I'm done',[20] he said. And now that the world is coming to an end, V., a curious voice, will ask Beckett, what will you say? 'Was there much of the journey you found worthwhile?' Answer: 'Precious little.' Two words. Untranslatable. *Qu'est-ce que ça valait, ce voyage? Bien peu. Pas grand-chose* (Not much). Precious little. Literally in French: *précieusement peu*. A fine idiomatic oxymoron. What is precious is little, precious little.

> [. . .] *'Precious little!'* But then a thought strikes him, and as if to contradict his own natural, now justified gloom, he directs us toward his second-best desk, collecting a bottle of whisky and glasses as he goes.[21]

Precious little. For Proust the five visitations: cobblestone spoon plate napkin water-pipe,[22] cup. The keys of his life-works. For his successor: skull, stick, sand, sky, grey, ray in the dark. The Almost-Nothings of the whole that make up the Whole.

4

Proust has just left. The cup remains. The cup passes to Beckett. A cup activated into a pot, as early as *Watt*, that is to say, into a hat, no, a bowler, or what, sexless, looks like a lowered chamber pot upside down and yellowed by time for had she never once appeared

> 24. V: For had she never once appeared, all that time, would I have, could I have, gone on begging, all that time? Not just vanished within my little sanctum and busied myself with something else, or with nothing, busied myself with nothing? Until the time came, with break of day, to issue forth again, shed robe and skull[cap], resume my hat and greatcoat, and issue forth again, to walk the roads.

> 25. *Dissolve to s empty. 2 seconds. M1 in robe and skullcap emerges from north shadow, advances five steps and stands facing camera. 2 seconds. He turns left and advances five steps to disappear in east shadow. 2 seconds. He emerges in hat and greatcoat from east shadow, advances five steps and stands facing west shadow. 2 seconds. He advances five steps to disappear in west shadow. 2 seconds.*

> 26. V: Right.[23]

That's what genius is about. First lines: last lines. Between both bits [*deux bouts*] that muddy bit of man

5

[*l'être de boue le boueux*] stretches in a dotted line for millions of minutes. Born nil [*Néant*]? Born in [*Né en*] 1906. Null, born in 1906. Nihilating today-as-yesterday, as a subject or figure or clown of time addicting himself, *addicted to the science of affliction*, the modern rehash of the science of *accidia*, this slow love of being, this slowness to love being, so slow, so low [*si lente, silence*], up to Hush![24] Never betrayed his edge, always remained on the side of the unbearable edge of the vase, slowly busying himself with the *constant process of decantation* [transvasement], vase, mud [*vase*], muddy and muddled [*vaseux*], *decantation from the vessel containing the fluid of future time, sluggish, pale and monochrome*,[25] 1929, 1930, today is already the dreary future stagnating the subject from one vase to another, the same vase later, now supine now kneeling, now a series in the dark, from one black darkness to another, with clasped knees, enters the head in between, now the head between the knees in the arms the head bowed down, it's well known, in 1985 as in 1930 same fable a little later, this time, same weary clasp a little less black thus never totally not black nor white. Sixty-five years of affliction through the decantation of a fable from A to F, *the fable of you fabling of one with you in the dark. And how better in the end labour lost and you as you always were.* Signed: *Seul* (alone). From right to left: *lues* (read).[26]

In Joyce's time in 1929 as well as in the time of *Company* in 1980, the cat chases its tail just as the fable

6

fables its tail in the dark as if it was another's. One touches oneself /one another, you bite yourself, I hear myself. This does not stop solitude. But still. Keeps it up. (*Pause.*)

Alone, the word. The word alone, alone, to sign and keep *company* to the depleter, self-depleting and self-depleted to the bone but only to the bone. For in order to be alone one must be more than one. Only the one who is accompanied, surrounded, pressed by solitude, feels alone. *Alone* keeps himself company *in the vicinity of zero*.

> There he opens then his eyes this last of all if a man and some time later threads his way to that first among the vanquished so often taken for a guide. [. . .] He himself after a pause impossible to time finds at last his place and pose whereupon dark descends and at the same instant the temperature comes to rest not far from freezing point [*dans le voisinage de zéro*]. Hushed in the same breath the faint stridulence mentioned above whence suddenly such silence as to drown all the faint breathings put together. So much roughly speaking for the last state of the cylinder and of this little people of searchers one first of whom if a man in some unthinkable past for the first time bowed his head if this notion is maintained.[27]

Whereas the Depleter opens his eyes once more maybe for the last time, like the last of the Marranos as

Jacques Derrida would say or like the last and the least of men if this is a man, as Jacques Derrida would say,[28] I believe I can hear the insistent echo of a salutation to the other neighbour of a zero of another kind, the one who in 1947 released the impossible, impassible portrait of the little depleted people, we all believe we can recognize the trace of Primo Levi, himself also the sober, Dantean minstrel of the most solitary solitudes of that century.[29] One will then believe one can recognize, devoured otherwise and similarly, the spectral, grotesque, doomed faces of 141,565 Elias Lindzin aliases, the monstrous, undecidable, extrahuman animalman who wound up at the *Lager*, Quasimodo unless it be Caliban,[30] or else even more unnamable than the unnamable[31] and almost totally exhumanused, one will see the very extinction of what was a man, now numbered, a pseudoman, all the rest having disappeared, lost name, no name, zero name, *Null Achtzehn* an endangered number about to disappear, a remainder: the last three digits of the prisoner's number, 018.

The furtive homage of one depeopled [*épeuplé*] man to another.

That's why I can love him, if this notion of loving can be maintained, for he maintains the being to faint in the vicinity of zero, himself Zero's Neighbour, without ever breaking, cancelling or betraying the difficult promiscuity, for a long time. For a long time.[32] All the time. It's long. What do we know about *long, short, brief, to end*? Brief long inexhaustible life of Proust long life abbreviation of Beckett.

It took us two thousand years to give a usable meaning to the thing *Neighbour* or *near*, what is *near*, nearby, the next (of kin), and we're not done yet.

– Your title says: *zero's neighbour*. Obviously you mean the *immediate* neighbour? There is not *one* neighbour. There is a neighbourhood or vicinity. In the vicinity of zero there is an infinity of neighbours. If you place yourself between -0.02 and 0.00002, you have a lot of people, the mathematician says.

– Let there be Zero's Neighbour. It hops. If Mr Beckett is Zero's neighbour, who is Zero? But Beckett may well be Zero. Zero's neighbour comes and pays him a visit. Zero's Neighbour tends towards Zero, he never gets there. There always remains a little something, 'precious little'.[33] A little something is no mean (no)thing, it is a little nothing, it is never nothing, one gets nearer, the Neighbour goes to Zero's, the null set. The Neighbour in the vicinity or his Voice.

V(O)ICINITY

Beckett against Metabeckett, with and against, right up against Metabeckett his text is full of voices, 'this I is

9

full of voices',[34] 'no trace anywhere of life, you say, pah, no difficulty there',[35] I say, imagination dead you say imagine I say, it [*ça*] speaks, a discourse within discourse and a discoursed disputed discourse, reality, he says, addressing the reader for two seconds, not more, for at the third second he breaks, the charm, I said reality but this is not it, let's get out of the book, one second, or rather no, let's go back in, let's say *reality* for the moment, although I don't know, and nor do you, what reality means, nor if there is any real one, for – he urges and drives us, to think, to despair, everything may just be an illusion, a simulacrum, not even fiction and a ploy. Top-class. Hats off. A question: what would one do without a hat [*chapeau*] in this metabeckettext? And. Without a cat [*chat*]? And without a skin [*peau*]? Man being a thinking hat.[36] No pure outside. No pure inside. No I without the other. No I without a pale other.

> I gave up before birth, it is not possible otherwise, but birth there had to be, it was he, I was inside, that's how I see it, it was he who wailed, he who saw the light, I didn't wail, I didn't see the light, it's impossible I should have a voice, impossible I should have thoughts, and I speak and think, I do the impossible, it is not possible otherwise, it was he who had a life, I didn't have a life, a life not worth having, because of me, he'll do himself to death, because of me, I'll tell the tale, the tale of his

10

death, the end of his life and his death, his death alone would not be enough, not enough for me, if he rattles it's he who will rattle, I won't rattle, he who will die, I won't die.[37]

Fizzle, he says. Foolery. Spoonery. All the gaffes and guff fizzling out.[38]

Not easy to be born [*naître*], worse to not be [*n'être*], to exit from life, all not easy, because of the cause. The cause: The one that caws [*La causeuse*]. The tongue with all its words everywhere even when aphasia, all these words, these letters, these traces everywhere stuck on the bone. It's not me! the child shouts. Me! Me, the echo answers. It's the old joke: We shout: Silence! Then not silence! Hush! Us? [*Chut! Chute?*] No silence. It takes all of Beethoven's music, he thinks, in order to create a gulp of silence.

The Beckett tongue with all its words, idioms, and parlances, all its acts, all its clichéd phenomena all pushed to the limit, to a crisis point, to excess, to the point of exasperation, sublimation, extra/ex/citation. Beckettese works through the fabulous scrambling of functions and differences, a way, unique in the world, of giving voice and primacy to what is always in our margins. Beckettese shelves and scraps the distinction between text and what is outside the text, the voice and what is outside the

11

voice, the said and the unsaid, spectacle and discourse. It cancels it. What is outside the frame enters the stage. The Stage Direction has its hour of glory. The mute line has its say. Since everything speaks. Speech speaks. Speech cuts itself short, apostrophizes itself, listens to itself, jokes itself. It smacks of quotation everywhere. And what are quoted infinitely quoted, quoted again, are turns of phrases. Instigator of the French-idiom, conjuractor of French snapshots, *monnaie courante* (common practice), *belle lurette* (donkey's years), and *à vrai dire* (actually), champion of parauditory deconstruction: that's what Beckettese forgery is. One has heard that already. It is something heard already that has become still-never-heard. Why this process?

A secret project of the writer's, secret to himself: *Taire* (to hush)! *Terre* (land ho)! He dreams of arriving where I is You. Creeps to the border [*bordure*]. Stages the walking alongside the border, till he starts wearing it down, tries to grind it down, just as the son grinds the father down after twenty years, border worn ordure, twenty years, still, (en)dure [-*dure*],[39] still, one text still after the other, one play after the other,

Wonders
What is the word [*Comment dire*[40]] for
'What is the word'

12

Without the word   'What is the Word' Poems

What is the way of doing away with the word, of ex-wording oneself, out-wording oneself [*comment s'exdire, s'horsdire*]

Out the word! But not from outside, if one needs an outside in order to jettison the word, to disown the word, to dis, to own [*pour se dédire de dire, pour se dé, pour se*], then one has to what is the word again [*tout est à recomment dire*],

Second attempt:

To call the word worse

Go on! worstward ho   Worstward Ho!

                                       Cap au pire[41]

Worse better than word

But still there's always worse.

So? So. No. (What would he do without no? I mean without No [*Non*]. Do you hear me: without noun [*nom*]. No point. No not. No. Oh, it does not know![42] One tries to escape but words wait for a chance to corner you. Round the bend [*coin*]. Round the dot [*point*].

Then one starts again. Order: Wortsward Ho

Worse [*pire*] better than hearse [*expire*]? Or conversely?

Oh! who hasn't dreamt of the worst, that is to say, of the best worst, that is to say, of the worst worst? Who, pursued by the intolerable pain of living alive, of being

13

lived alive by life, of being bitten alive by death, has not dreamt of a limit to pain, for there is no end, no end but variations of pain and inventions of pain, to live that is to say, to be alive *in* life, that is to say, to be in suffering, to be the everlasting letter in sufferance, the everlasting being [*l'être sempiternel*], the worstless being [*l'être sans pis*], the letterless jester of being [*le pitre sans lettre d'être*], to live, that is to say, to be the being *in*, the being inside in front/owing [*devant*], that is to say, *in* other words in pain, to feel that, *the being in pain*, and no end, only changes of pain, among which, among the worst, maybe the worst, if there was one (but what a triumph it would be if there was something one day, if there was, or happened, but no, out of the question), the worst maybe, I was saying, would be the unknown pain, the ghost pain, the muffled roar in the skull, the breath of nothingness, no, the breath of a nothingness, murmuring what if I didn't exist? if even I wasn't, if not even nothingness *for* you, if nothing else than you less than nothingness, you're less than nothingness, can you imagine? – the phantom pain, that is to say, the pain of never being able to taste the end, never counting on the end for there is no final end, only the interminable drawing out of an ever-ending [*finissance*] which courses through the blood back to the brain cells and all of life is in truth nothing but this *nihilating*, this undoing of each day by each day,

14

I come back to my initial sigh: Oh! who hasn't dreamt of the worst, for when one generally mentions it, the worst is what is simplest, what is most desirable, for the worst is the name for the best, it is death, no, not to die, I do mean death, but one will never have death, one dreams about it, one calls it, waits for it, there are some who even give it names, some call it Godot, or Go, go, or gozzo, etc. Who, which poor creature doomed to live, which human, which egoist, which egodoist hasn't dreamt of the super worst, of the good worst, of the soft worst [*doux pire*], of the end, of the end of all worsts, of sighs suspiring and surspiring [*des soupirs, des surpires*], a truly real end, the one that is waved like a carrot (I take the carrot in Vladimir's pocket and naturally it's a turnip) in front of Moses' nose in order to make him walk to the barrier of the promised one, for Moses is the first in literature to have had the frightful experience of life without end, without final(e), that is to say, of life, that is to say, of life reduced [*vie amputée*], of this deuced life [*amputée de vie*[43]] that is done to us, made of successive, varied reductions [*amputations*], of lessenings and parings, for God knows we have a lot of them to lose, God knows that, in order to come almost at an end [*venir à presque à bout*], for there is no end, anyway who is talking about being an end [*être de bout*], I mean being on end [*debout*], not being of mud [*de bou*e], yes, so, in order to come almost at an end, it's mad, it's maddening

15

what has to be given over to the torturer, *the torturer*, hey, Hamm would be pleased to have found him! *One can always lose still more*, that's the law of living, to live, that is to say, to always still lose and without ever being able to hope to gain/reach the end at least:

> Pozzo: I don't seem to be able. . . [*He hesitates.*]. . . to depart.
> Estragon: Such is life.

> *Silence.*
> Pozzo. – Je n'arrive pas. . . (il hésite). . . à partir.
> Estragon. – C'est la vie.[44]

That pain be *live* and that the thing-beings be extremely alive, terribly, cruelly alive, in Beckett's Dantean tent, nobody can doubt it. For contrary to what one might think, all these inhabitants, of different natures, all the animated species incarcerated in his expurgatory, are restless, feverish, loquacious, no matter how deloquacified or shortened they may be, ceaselessly connected, brought backwards, taken back, commanded, agitated no matter how paralysed they may be, over-excited by life's parasitic interference, self-reflexified, self-galvanized, submitted to the process called Life, in the grip of the virus of Life (and thus never dead, there is nothing but life), of this strange, frightening genetic evil spell which produces

16

individuals who are designated either by names or by signs, it's almost the same, run through by excitements and all, whether they be present one way or another or absent one way or another, partly or wholly, on one stage or another, all in an agonistic phase, all agonists, all tossed like the miserable remains of pathetic gladiators into an arena of autoheteromangling.

The extraordinary energy freed by these dregs and masses in order to take three steps, not to take a single step, to fight like ancient lions only left with one fang to get near something like a window [*fenêtre*] which will naturally win dough [*fait feu de tout naître*], but takes on, for all those sensitive to the promise of the thing and of the signifier, the importance, say, of a cathedral for Goethe, and which however is nothing but a casement pencilled on a wall – this energy is ours. We recognize it. While moaning we recognize ourselves in this numb [*mate*] suffering. Checkmate [*Échec et mat*]. Check (and) Mate are the two characters of the lost play by Sam (and) Beckett. Poor pawns that we are, that is to say, poor clown of the regal characters we once were only in the past of another world.

What energy of a shrunken giant, in order *(not)* to make or take a *step*, for the quantity of energy is not measured according to the object to be made, or by referring to an anthropometry or a classical anthropology. In order to take a step one centimetre, one millimetre, one word, three dots short, one needs a nuclear energy, in order to *make* an image, to make, to make the least, to make. Beckett, like Dante, as a precursor of nanostructures, of the immense powers of nano-beings. Beckett, like Freud, as an astrophysicist of the dramaticules of interior chaosmos.[45]

Here, there, under the skull, small is big, a matter of the glance of an eye.

Seen unseen illseen a matter of (non)seeing [*question de pointdevue*], looked-at notseen wellillseen by seeing otherwise unseeing O'Eye,[46] by Milton *Agonistes'* glaucous O'Eye,[47] by Joyce's glaucomat O'Eye,[48] by Beckett's blind eagle O'Eye, by blindeagle O'Eye [*Œil d'avaigle*], O, the object, the object O, zero, grows, disproportionately, one in the eye for you [*en met plein la vue*]. Beckett posthuming Joyce. Joyce prophesying Sam's arrival. Foreseeing, anticipating. One day one could read all of the ill-seeing Beckett as a *fauxbondir*[49] to the blind James Joyce.

He wants to see nobody. (I will relate my encounter with Beckett in the dark, not here, one of these days)

Seenillseen thoughtseen

through the leucoma the Obstacle O is titanic.

All those who struggle in order to raise a ton of eyelids, ten tons of legs, who must stir the whole sand beach bordering the town in order to extract a step while the townspeople run on ordinary legs, are Dante's and therefore Beckett's natural readers. Suffering is not what the man said to be 'in good health' believes it to be. Behind the suffering there is a smithy. In this smithy *tiredness*, humanity's worst enemy, is manufactured with much huffing and puffing. I mean humanity as a species and humanity as a virtue.

'I WAS WEARY WHEN I BEGAN',[50] I say, he says, one says. Already I was weary [*las*] when I began. Already I was here [*là*] when I began. To begin with I was here, otherwise no beginning. Alas [*hélas*] to begin weary, to wearybegin, to disbegin to begin with. I was already here to begin with [*pour commencer*]. Afterwards how it is (to begin) [*comment c'est*], comedy, not company, no, no com-, no commencement, no company, all already, weary. I begin again, I try, I try to try and begin, impossible, without being weary, to try to begin before, to begin a virgin beginning was the dream of Jacques Derrida to begin impossible life to try, how it is, is it, etc., to begin again, for in order to end again one must indeed begin, etc.

I resume, voice A said: I was weary when I began. I am not surprised. You thought, I thought. It's normal. One must indeed be here in order to begin. How tiring! Normal. Norming.[51] Inaugural. Oh yes, and you believed, you believe, that A is him, is me, who says I was here when I began. Truce to suspense. And if I truce

19

it is only because we are in the house of a theatre, hence finite, theatres are finite and they finish. One is going to finish and exit. But if I was in a book, hence non finite, finishing all the time never finished, then no truce, truce of truce, no truce would ever abolish suspense and truce. But, I resume, we are in the house of a theatre, A said: I was weary when I began.

A, that is to say, B, you're thinking, that is to say, Beckett, it is indeed B such a statement, you say to yourself, although it may be Y, that is to say you, or C, that is to say me, and unquestionably H, that is to say, Human. What is beautiful, please note, is the past historic which you did not hear, but you can believe me the sentence said: *je commençai* (I began), with *ai*. Here it becomes interesting, I resume therefore: the day, the hour, the minute, the page, the line, the strophe when I began for the first time, I thought, but who knows when to begin begins, first, I was weary, here and tired beforehand of what follows [*suit*] and would follow, of what I am [*suis*] and will be, therefore tired of what I will have been before being here and after as well. As we are in a theatre, I cut out the twenty pages which follow this one.[52] We climb inside the cleft rock (this rock is in the twenty pages I have skipped), whose walls press against us on either side, and the ground that we tread, and which is steep though laid on paper, needs both hands and feet, which we could designate by RH, LH, etc., as you know. You

20

recognize. To all four limbs, to which the cleft rock, the book, the text, compel us to resort, a fifth one, a stick, another, can be added. There are also the belly and the knees. Well. Flat on one's belly, as they say, seen from the belly the summit is so high that the sight cannot reach it and the slope far steeper than the one the line from the circle's centre makes with the mid-quadrant – here a long silence – of exhaustion – I cut short – our – interrogations. Enough erring.

A, the voice, isn't B's voice, no, although. Is a bit mine since I lent it to him, to A, long enough to pronounce, caress, quote, I was here to say *I was here* [là] *when I began.* I will add that this sentence could also be found in my own writings, but to begin with, I *nicked and stitched* it,[53] as Jacques Derrida would say, on the stony path which does not lead to San Leo, nor to Bismantova,[54] nor to Dublin, nor; but, yes, leads to Purgatory. Where are we, now on the meridian where those who crawl for all those who are inside or in front or behind, or who come later, skid instead of us, for us, there's no mystery, there's only a bit of a gap, a bit of substitution, he was weary when I began, who, the predecessor and naturally the follower, each weary for the other and each for themselves and because. Before me you, before you him before and consequently. Before me, that is to say, you and me, Beckett, before whom Dante before him Belacqua, each self, each me, and everybody on all fours, for seen from where we are, (your) stumps of me, if there'a summit our eyesight does not reach it, if there's an entrance, if there is an exit for stumps there is only the word for exit. However, one can always imagine a voice saying: Drag yourself over here. Let's imagine: *Drag yourself over here*, says Voice V(irgil).[55] And it shows me an overhang which, on this side but not on the other, skirts round the whole of the mountain, you see. These words spur me so well that with one arguably titanic effort I caught up with V on all fours, so that I had the ledge under my feet. If one does not have a ledge under one's feet, says Kafka, one must invent it with one's feet, scratch the ground with one's toes. Acrobat. Likewise Beckett. Likewise Dante.

Let's move on. The weary one that begins does not begin with Beckett, with B. The weary one is Dante. That canto has got enough to be weary about. And enough not be weary about yet for, as we know, it is in the *ante*, in the *Ante-Purgatory*. Just imagine. Neither Inferno nor Purgatory. Between and before. Now, when one has got used to this ante-place nowhere before, colourless if not white or all in a dotted outline, one will recognize the boards of Beckett's world, that stage where one finds it difficult to stand for in the long run it is nothing but edge and ledge, a cleft in the rock, white rotunda in the whiteness[56] diameter eighty centimetres barely enough to make a world without ornament, without islands without waters, remains word scrap of word, rhyme,

22

echo of a step, no step [*pas de pas*], echo, co, o, no void, the void promises, worse: fullness everywhere, a ring full no place for me a ring as in the imagination the ring of bone. The ring of bone, remains of the horn, I mean remains of Roland's oliphant, of which only remains end of the world, alone, bone, o [*monde, onde, os, o*].

I come back to Purgatory in which in fact I have remained, for their Purgatory, that of Dante, Beckett and their likes, stretches all round Purgatory, at the foot, before, in imagination, all is Purgatory. Always already in order to begin before having begun, ante Beckett, when still not cut off from Joyce, already Purgatory, to me Purgatory.

> In what sense, then, is Mr Joyce's work purgatorial? In the absolute absence of the Absolute. [. . .] There is a continuous purgatorial process at work, in the sense that the vicious circle of humanity is being achieved, and this achievement depends on the recurrent pre-domination of one of two broad qualities.
>
> [. . .] On this earth that is Purgatory, Vice and Virtue – which you may take to mean any pair of large contrary human factors – must in turn be purged down to spirits of rebelliousness. Then the dominant crust of the Vicious or Virtuous sets, resistance is provided, the explosion duly takes place and the machine proceeds. And no more than this; neither prize nor penalty;

simply a series of stimulants to enable the kitten to catch its tail. And the partially purgatorial agent? The partially purged.[57]

Now for a human quadrupedicle there is nothing more infernal than personal Purgatory.

When they go, the great artists of the imagination leave among us immortal creatures, unheard-of and the likes of us, who from now on help us recognize the thorny paths where we suddenly find ourselves captive. These beings become our masters and our initiators [*passeurs*], they live forever among us, lame, anguished, grotesque, representative of our fatalities and thus reassuring. Kafka leaves us K., Joyce Stephen Dedalus and Bloom, Stendhal the twins Fabrice and Julien, Flaubert Saint Julian, Clarice Lispector G. H. No time to evoke them all. And Beckett? Belacqua. It is by this – shabby [*miteux*], mythical – legacy of the being he will have left us and the state in which he will have left him that I recognize Beckett's peculiar genius among them all. His survivor, his delegate, his residue, his spectre, his used-up double, his nilanticipator, his foreshadower, his forerunner [*devancier*] and sometime [*ci-devant*] friend,[58] the model for his thousand self-portraits of the artist as a Thingummy *frozen and collapsing endlessly, sinfully indolent, bogged in indolence.*[59] Thingummy, whatsit, that,

24

whowhichwhatever it might be, everything is (1) in the position in space, such as it is described one hundred and forty-seven times in Beckett's textual gallery, a foetal, fatal deconstruction before the letter of phallogocentric erection; (2) in stagnation in time.

Quite some find it was, this almost-nobody, invisible at first glance, a voice behind a big block of stone, which makes itself heard like an inner voice, contradicting Virgil, prophesying to Dante the collapse on his rear, quite some find it was, this untamed creature, slouched, on reprieve, parasite, brother and incarnation of the strangest passion that might affect a human being: sloth, *pigritia*. As Kafka has known since Dante, man has lost and cannot regain Paradise out of sloth. Negative passion. Others would say *resistance*.

A paradox: in order to find Belacqua, one must have overcome sloth and negligence.

And yet there is in Beckett a Belacqua who raises his head just enough to say: Brother, why bother ascending? since the divine bird sitting on the threshold of the gate would not let me go to punishments? – A man persevering in sloth, this Belacqua is. A self-befizzled [*autoenfoiré*], Beckett would say.

> *Là ci traemmo; e ivi eran persone*
> *Che si stavano a l'ombra dietro al sasso*
> *Come l'uom per negghienza a star si pone.*

E un di lor, che mi sembiava lasso,
Sedeva e abbracciava le ginocchia,
Tenendo 'l viso giù tra esse basso.
'O dolce segnior mio', diss'io, 'adocchia
colui che mostra sé più negligente
che se pigrizia fosse sua serocchia.'
Allor si volse a noi e puose mente,
movendo 'l viso pur su per la coscia,
e disse: 'Or va tu sù, che se' valente!'

Thither we approached, and there were persons strown
In postures at the rock's back in the shade
Listless as one who for his rest sinks down.
And one, whose looks the weariness betrayed,
With hands clasping his knees was sitting there,
And had his forehead low between them laid.
'O sweet my Lord', said I, 'turn thine eyes here
Upon that one who more indifferent shows
Himself than if Sloth were his own sister.'
Then, seeming to give heed, he turned to us,
Moving his face only over his thigh,
And said: 'Go up now, thou who art valorous!' [60]

One needs to have read all of Joyce and all of
Dante, Homer, Proust, the Bible, to have descended into
Inferno and *a hundred times* [cent fois], that is to say,
without [*sans*] the help of faith [*foi*], walked round the

base of Purgatory in order to find at the bottom of canto IV the few lines which give the Sin of Sloth its minute immortal hero. And if Beckett had not stooped to pick him up with a tiny smile curling at the corner of his lips, he would have remained neglected forever.

Belackett's great readers are the greatly tired, the great explorers of those grey regions (of the grey Beckett), penumbras [*pénombres*], shadows pining for [*ombres en peine de*] a body, for joy, the artists of tiredness, those who all the time or for a while, or from time to time, dwell in the fearful kingdom. You can see I am thinking of Gilles Deleuze here, whose tiredness I saw more than once, from very close and thus yet from very far. How not to forcefully write 'The Exhausted', an inexhaustible shared theme. Besides there is no exhaustion in Beckett, 'The Exhausted' is Gilles Deleuze's signature. It is also a formidable text which attempts to master the ugly enemy, slimy and tattery, 'who tries to make resistance yield'. Beckett in the role of the exhauster of the exhausting, that is to say, of the inexhaustible, and more precisely the Exhauster, by vocation and occupation, of all the inexhaustibles, *one* after *the other*.

One will eventually have to begin to understand that the Exhauster takes on the successive inexhaustibles only in the secret hope of reaching exhaustion, in other words self-exhaustion, in other words the impossible.

Beckett's text is perfectly clear: it is a question of exhausting space. There is no doubt that the characters will become tired, and will drag their feet more and more. Yet tiredness primarily concerns a minor aspect of the enterprise: the number of times one possible combination is realized (for example, two of the duos are realized twice, the four trios twice, the quartet four times). The characters become tired depending on the number of realizations. But the possible is accomplished, independently of this number, by the exhausted characters who exhaust it. The problem is: in relation to what is exhaustion (which must not be confused with tiredness) going to be defined?[61]

I said there is no exhaustion, and this is what exhausts but not exhaustively, what tires out but not terminally, the exhauster and the reader or the spectator who enters into sympathy or into identification.

Knackering the animal. Gruelling the reader. Lucky, reader. Think! Forward! Stop! Back! There! On![62] On! On: the most cruel word, Jean-Jacques Mayoux[63] used to say.

Knackering the animal knackers the knackerer. The tirer tires. To tire, here is a verb which contains all the resources of passion without having to use the pronominal form.

Lucky is tired. Estragon is tired. Pozzo is tired.

VLADMIR: [*To* POZZO.] You don't complain?

POZZO: I'm tired.

[*Silence.*]

ESTRAGON: Nothing happens, nobody comes, nobody goes, it's awful![64]

Tired. . .

by whom? By whom and by what.

VLADIMIR: You're being asked a question.

POZZO: [*Delighted.*] A question! *Who*? What? A moment ago you were calling me Sir, in fear and trembling. Now you're asking me questions. No good will come of this!

VLADIMIR: [*To* ESTRAGON.] I think he's listening.

ESTRAGON: [*Circling about* LUCKY.] What?

VLADIMIR: You can ask him now. He's on the alert.

ESTRAGON: Ask him *what*?[65]

Fidelity to tiredness, fidelity of the artist, like Kafka's Hunger Artist, the *Hungerkünstler* will have been faithful to hunger till the fulfilment of hunger.

The onus is still on us to work out the negative, the positive is already given to us. Kafka has some faith remaining. Beckett: no faith remaining.

One of the first signs of incipient knowledge is the wish to die. This life appears unbearable, another

29

unattainable. One is no longer ashamed of wanting to die; one begs to be moved from the old cell, which one hates, to a new one, which one will then learn to hate. At work in this is a remainder of faith that, during the move, the master will chance to come along the corridor, look at the prisoner [. . .].[66]

A paradox: the exhauster is tireless, tiredness is inexhaustible. Whoever knows tiredness will have tasted the bitter process of successive weakening, slow overweakcoming [*accablissement*], the lassitudinal experience of the diminution of strengths together with the augmentation of weaknesses,

the rubbing of jaws diminution/augmentation the entanglement of contraries which produces an oscillation which produces a reduction which increases towards the end without ever reaching the final point

Naught not best worse. Less best worse. No. Least. Least best worse. Least never to be naught. Never to naught be brought. Never by naught be nulled. Unnullable least. Say that best worst. With leastening words say least best worse.[67]

'Hiatus for when the disappeared words', the text preterites.

These 'authors' who are employed by the secret Law

30

of literature, born devoted to the outside, each accomplish their task in the place where fate set them down, workers of a babblical tower which they spend their lives constructing ruining, construining, each completing their masterpiece, putting to death, in their place, each their own nut and bolt, all take on the God gate, the Tower, Kafka's lot will have been to receive the Emperor of China's message,[68] he does not know which emperor is ruling, but sat at the window of his book, he dreams endlessly this message which may have to do with the building of the Great Wall – which perhaps for the first time in the history of humanity was to provide the solid base for a new tower of Babel, but nobody still nowadays knows how to imagine the building of the tower.

Beckett's lot will have been to tire the end, to imagine how to tire it to imagine in vain *the end of the end*.

How long dying is, it doesn't come, it doesn't end, what a story! as they say, *never finished anything, everything always went on for ever.*[69]

What he uses up while trying to use himself up is discourse, it falls to shreds. . . and it lasts, using up duration, what an idea, what a life!

You're not exactly short of inertia, bad will, awkwardness, bad faith – though there's a bit of all that, for 'vermin is bred from nothingness' (Kafka would say, Bernhard would say), which makes you fail, which does not even

31

make you fail in everything: love, friendship, life as a parent, life as a child, occupation: without, no occupation, nobody – it is the lack of end, of end and *of end*, doubly, one and the other, for both are linked, one makes the other, yes the end makes the end, the end of one makes the end of man, and the lack of end, thus of a limit, thus of finality as well, is like the lack of air and the lack of law, it's unliveable with. Now this unliveable, nothing doing, needs to be lived, since one is not out of the horrible wood, by inches [*à petit feu*], with the paltry means at one's disposal, that is to say, it needs to be unlived, one must hold on, make a bit of soil, a bit of air, a bit of law, Kafka would say *create*, but not Beckett, no, not create, make up, patch up, not in order to be able to catch up on what you neglected, one cannot catch up on what precedes us, but in order to weave and unweave the duration of time, for this task, well, is as good as another.

It seems and it appears that any human being (let's call that *human* and that *being*, but sometimes that is called subject, or object, or thing) should be able to or can justify his life or his death which comes down to the same thing, should he be doing nothing else, have no occupation, no home, he would not escape that one task, nothing else but at least. Being must needs admit being, answering therefore, at least, the least man, for that which *he is* at least, and which he has not yet, still *not finished being yet*. What is Being doing there? It does.

What? *Quaqua? (How It Is)*[70] The essential. Not more. Not less. *Whew.*[71] For example. (That's untranslatable, isn't it? To whew. Who can do so only in English. Same for to whoa [*faire Œuf*], or to whoosh [*faire feu*]. But in each language one will wangle a way to whew otherwise.) Just in English. We note: to whew! or to *phew*! whew (it's all in the intonation, and one should, but I don't have the time, interpret-read 'Beckett', 'the work', as they always say, on at least two tones, on a *whew* of pain and on a *whew* of relief. Thus, for *Embers* and *Words and Music*, etc. or an anguished version, a saved version, separately, both at the same time, in succession, etc.). *Ouf!*

I come back to the 'essential'. *To live?* What was astonishing is that we could see any human being live or die his life, it's the same. Now, without an inner *justification*, this result would not be possible. I am repeating Kafka's philosophical astonishment here: a kind of living? Who's talking about living? No being can live an unjustified life. Every man seemingly works in order to feed, etc. In secret for each visible mouthful he receives an invisible mouthful, and this invisible mouthful is the justification of any human being. And justification is a belated construction, a psychological gimmick, a mirror effect, Kafka would say, the mystery called life drive, Freud would say, one cannot not do, one is not free not to, after which one invents, but in secret, without doing it on purpose, or consciously, a justification which one believes in, the

33

simulacrum of a law which one obeys, and a whole raft of illusions, which in the end, by sheer dint of believing [*à force et à force d'être crues*], eventually become some kinds of realities sound enough for me to be able to place my body in them in a sitting position, or lying, or straddling a bicycle or writing a book. Naturally, this psychical, indispensable operation, this sheer drudgery of a work [*travail de forçat*] whose end, whose (unavowed) goal is to give oneself enough means to believe that one cannot do otherwise than believe, to give oneself, to believe oneself, etc. *on the one hand* is threatened at any moment from the inside and from the outside of being suddenly unmasked as a sham, and this would be a catastrophe, one would crumble instantly to salt and dust, *on the other hand* calls on extraordinarily resilient strengths [*forces*], which act as ability of what I am not able to, as power of lack of power, but at the cost of a ruinously expensive duel.

Whereas one is dying to be dead, when the time is young and thus bad.

> ADA: And why life? [*Pause.*] Why life, Henry? [*Pause.*] Is there anyone about?[72]

Youremember, the time the good old one, when one was dying to be dead? No difference, except the price of margarine

In the meantime it's mad how much the price of

margarine has increased. Youremember fifty years ago, that is to say, five hundred years it's the same and nowadays, the price of BlueBand! nowadays! It's always the same, isn't it? *per aspera ad astra*,[73] the same difficulties, that is to say, the same paths always changing in the space which never changes, it was already like that in Joyce's time, that is to say, the same thing as in the time of Pliny and Columella,[74] that is to say, in the time of birds as well as in the time of aeroplanes,

now tell me, Henry, did you know Ada? Ada? never known Ada, did you, yes, no. Ada is the a(u)ditress, the ear and the speech, sympathizing, as tender as margarine, never mind, without Ada, impossible, one would have to invent her otherwise who could one complain to about all this, starting with Ada. Ada, not Adam, Ada was is and will be that,[75] Hell, to talk-cause [*causer*] with her, chit-chatting, to remember the good old time when one was dying to be dead, Ada always the same from left to right or from right to left palindrome

To live?

And why life? It's meaningless. Life, the question.

So why life? Is there anyone about? Not a single cat,[76] you might say. It's meaningless to drown a cat if there ever was one

– No, then no why [*pourquoi*], then *quaqua*, then how?

– How life, tell me, Henry, tell me, Joe, Winnie, Hamm, tell me, Krapp.[77]

– I do my utmost to do.

To do. To do what? Well, a hole, for instance – and even more than a hole, as in *Embers*.

The hole is still there. Where we did it at last for the first time.

> HENRY: [. . .] [*Pause.*] The hole is still there, after all this eternity. [*Pause. Louder.*] The hole is still there.
> ADA: What hole? The earth is full of holes.
> HENRY: Where we did it at last for the first time.
> ADA: Ah yes, I think I remember. [*Pause.*] The place has not changed.[78]

The hole is still there after.

The hole is still always already there before.

So many holes in a few moments, a few lines.

One agrees with Ada: there are all the holes there, the earth is full of them. And what about time then? Nothing but holes.

A pause in time is also an eternity. An empty time is an eternity.

Time has a finite duration as long as it is full. The moment you take an empty time, you have all the hole.

The hole is still there after an eternity.

Between you and me, the Earth is above all a feminine

element. The earth is *full* and *has holes*. The feminine is the hole and what is full. – Where did we do it? – In a hole. – Ah yes, I think I remember, I have a hole.

And what is there as a cosmic hole? There's nothing but that, all the cosmological theories are full of Holes, the Black Hole, in a way a bound distortion, is a well in which there is no more space even. Before the Big Bang, the moment when space is born, the greatest nothingness of the nothingness of the nothingness would be 'before' the Big Bang but before there is no before. Hole.

What would the hole be?

The hole is not even nothingness, it is the *place of nothingness*, even a full hole is still a hole.

After any eternity there is still space.

One holes something. One *makes* a hole: irruption of nothingness into matter (irruption of space) of not full into what's full.

The hole is *negative* rather than *nil*.

The hole of 'the time [*la fois*]'. It took some time in doing. For years one has been away at it. But one got there in the end. One did it in the end.

To do = to put in some time, to make the hole, to put some time in the hole, to make a hole in time

– To do? – (There goes) the proof.

Even a tiny little possible, the tiniest possible of the possibles, is the proof.

The tiniest possible of the tiniest possibles that I can

do my utmost to do is imagination dead, is to imagine still to image, to murmur, to phew, to ph.;[79] *ouf*, enough, nuff. Sufflive. Suvive [*ça suffit. Suffivre. Survivre*].

Still, life, *all id* is that is [tout ça *tout ce ça*], all that nothing, is extraordinary, Winnie said so, how wonderful, all that there is in the bag, of life, all M. and Mme Jourdain have done life without knowing it.[80] Pass me your handkerchief o life! Life of worms, nothing but head and no butt, head to butt, nothing but.[81]

What am I saying, life of *old* worms, for, let's not forget, all these inhabitants, corpuscles, slavemaster-slaves, have time, it can be seen in the word *old*, if the style is *old*, and if Winnie has the *old* prayer, it is because time blows [*souffle*] on these old worms. And not only. Let's take *Happy Days*. Just the last pages in French, there are twenty-seven *pauses* in time [temps] between brackets. Seven outside. All in all three hundred and seventy-nine pauses outside, five hundred and thirteen inside.[82]

> WINNIE: Or just now and then [*de temps en temps*], come round this side just every now and then and let me feast on you. [*Back front.*] But you can't, I know. [*Head down.*] I know. [*Pause. Head up.*] Well anyway – [*looks at toothbrush in her hand*] – can't be long now – [*looks at brush*] – until the bell. [*Top back of* WILLIE's *head appears above slope.* WINNIE *looks closer at brush.*]

Fully guaranteed. . . [*head up*] . . . what's this it was? [WILLIE*'s hand appears with handkerchief, spreads it on skull, disappears.*] Genuine pure. . . fully guaranteed. . . [WILLIE*'s hand appears with boater, settles it on head, rakish angle, disappears*] . . . genuine pure. . . ah! hog's setae. [*Pause.*] What is a hog exactly? [*Pause. Turns slightly towards* WILLIE.] What exactly is a hog, Willie, do you know, I can't remember. [*Pause. Turning a little further, pleading.*] What is a hog, Willie, please! [*Pause.*]

[. . .]

WINNIE: Oh this is a happy day! This will have been another happy day! [*Pause.*] After all. [*Pause.*] So far. [*Pause.* [. . .] WILLIE *turns page. Pause. He turns another page. Pause.*][83]

By *pauses* here I mean the *temps* or 'times' that take place between brackets, in italics, which can be read in the book, which are played onstage, which are said in *French*, for in English there are no *times*, instead of time(s), there is an interruption, there is a *pause*,

Happy Days is a play in two acts, in two tongues in French, that is to say, a play in two stages [*à double temps*], bisextual, half spoken, half scanned, half words, half interval, half expanse of scorched grass, half space of time held between clasped hands. Is a prayer with after-prayer, preprayer, postprayer. A prayer play with

39

two puppets and a main spectral prompter, actor, character, *souffleur*. Imagine the master, not onstage, the inaudible whisperer with his metronome, the surveyor of metres, centimetres, millimetres of time, imagine Sam with his bag of hours, that is to say, sixty minutes, let's say, in Roman type, loud voice and symmetrically sixty *mimutes*, that is to say, sixty units of mime, tongue of other signs, tongue two, tongue the other

If one takes *the trouble to read*, for instance the inscription on the handle of a toothbrush (said to be 'the last object', that is, the brush with ghostly teeth), one will be at it for a very long time, in order to meditate fully a whole philosophy, genuine, pure, guaranteed, what is truth, what is purity, guard [*la garde*], etc. (not to mention the hog in the end, thus quite the opposite of the pure, isn't it, and what about the setae, all that on the handle of a toothbrush – the avatar of Hamlet's nutshell[84])

There's no change rhymes with *it is strange*, it's marvellous, this nothing that changes except the affect of the speaking subject, now the day is beautiful, now the day, the same day, is worse, or white or black, it's the same otherwise, 'being', an accentuation-diminution till *ping*.[85] *Ping* portrait of a skeleton with unknown skull bonce by an unknown painter. From Winnie to Ping, from the tumulus to the tomb-like white, they do nothing but melt.

40

So how do you fare in French when you want to make do [*faire faire*].[87] *Faire* je dis *faire*, I say. I do say: I say (I) do [*je dis faire*]. Homophone in French: *je diffère* (I defer/differ). Yes I do, I do say all this in French indeed.[88] Everything I say, everything I say I do and defer/differ when I say *dis faire* and *diffère*, here, today, *is in French*. I repeat. For everything would be different if I said, did and deferred/differed in English. I *dis*, *fais* and *diffère* in French, including the errors, mine as well as Beckett's, those conscious as well as unconscious. The errors I will make in French, I would not be able to make them in English, and the other way round, I would make others. Then I will correct them, in French if in French, in English if in English.

As I am doing all this in French in front of you, I am still not being unfair [*infidèle*] to Beckett, not more not less than him. I won't have the time here to do a paper, an *essai*, a lecture, a *communication* on the issue of the language that was given up, not quite, run away from and spat out by Beckett, the mother tongue spat out of his mouth as soon as possible, very quickly very soon, in the 1920s, but this lecture, *communication*, reflection must exist and it does exist, it is in secret here, in reserve, and spread everywhere beneath each page and in each sentence, since in spite of appearances[89] I am addressing myself to you in French, the language elected by Beckett after few hesitations, which does not prevent one from stepping or passing [*pas de passer*] from one edge to the other from E to F and from F to E, depending on the setup, a lure effe-effect[90] guaranteed for the reader, and all for the son of a ben-effit[91] of the scriptor Ltd. In his shoes I would do exactly the same. Let me say two words about this here. If only for the word *pas*,[92] the French language is well worth it, when all is said and done. Just imagine no *pas* in English,[93] thus no step farther with *pas*, that is to say, *pas de pas*, imagine the English stepping in its p(l)ace and taking *pas* in its stride, it barely walks, does it [*ça ne va pas trop n'est-ce pas*], imagine 'not', 'step', 'pace', 'stride', 'gait', 'walk',[94] and I pass up others, whereas so much passes with and in a French *pas*, even a pah!, in one and the same *pas* all the universe and all philosophy in two words, not even/even not [*même pas*].

And what about *sans* (without) then? What would he do withoutless, bloodless hundredless by the name of less[95] how to make do with less [*s'en passer*]? This ashen [*de cendres*] taste, this word *sans*, which appealed even to Shakespeare. 'Sans teeth sans eyes sans taste sans everything'[96] you remember.

Just take a look at the two false twin volumes of *Harrap's Dictionary* or another and Sam's appetite for the lean is effectively done for [*c'est en fait*], just put side by side the thin F.E. whereas in comparison E.F. is twice as big fat thick heavy [*gros gras lourd lard*] proliferating voluminous, naturally, and so to speak, congenitally, Beckett, poor him, has been on the side of the effete [*efflanqué*][97] ever since his first steps, first words, first (non-)step words [*pas de mots*] he will have chosen the more economical language straightaway, the French language is less meaty and looks lean,[98] so does he, tall lean and as athletic. French has fewer words. It has a more limited vocabulary than English. The words serve more purposes, that's what he needs, to privilege the syntactical and lexical formulas of abstraction. French is his diet and his regime. To look leaner and leaner, ever fasting.

I have now come back to the *principle* of the whole work, to the decisive decision which drives and moves the circles, cylinders, circuits of the ring in the Sam Beckett circus. The point is to cut [*tailler*] and to cut and run [*se tailler*], to burst open the continuums, to bring the silences to justice and make them disgorge. The Beckett-literature is already proclaimed by Belacqua in 1932. Sam is twenty-six years old, he precedes himself, announces himself prophesies himself. He will be the rough, rugged minstrel of the literature of the *Unwort*, that is to say, of the *Unword*, that is to say, of the *immot*. An admirable precursor of himself. Since the secret manifests of his private texts, already since *Dream of Fair to Middling Women* and since the famous letter to Axel Kaun in 1937, a letter written *in German* to one of his mates, his own Seer's letter,[99] the revolutionary's letter, the worldwide proclamation to a single listener, he will have promised his coming to a work unheard of and *in French*. His desire, his programme, is to go and distance himself as far as possible from the English language from the soft-sounding Engluish [*l'engluanglais*], while coming as near as possible to the Ante-French, diamanté and cutting, Racine's razor-sharp steel [*l'acéré acier de Racine*], Rimbaud's breathtaking pace, and on top of that the bistro cant from the rue Saint-Jacques. He has the ear. He is the ear. Precocious. One can understand why he kept aloof in the vicinity of Mr Joyce, too near and so absolutely antithetically other. One had to be strong, cunning, and. . . Protestant in order to resist the excatholic Ulyssean siren. Two words about the letter in German, written to himself of course, care of Axel Kaun as they say. Why this annunciatory monument of *the flight from Egypt*, that is to say, the crossing towards the promised French language, without trembling, in German? Why French and not German? I have my own idea. No time to answer here today. Time is pressing us.

I'd rather give words and music back to him – too briefly –

> The uniform, horizontal writing, flowing without accidence, of the man with a style, never gives you the margarita. But the writing of, say, Racine or Malherbe,

perpendicular, diamanté, is pitted, is it not, and sprigged with sparkles; the flints and pebbles are there, no end of humble tags and commonplaces. They have no style, they write without style, do they not, they give you the phrase, the sparkle, the precious margaret. Perhaps only the French can do it. Perhaps only the French language can give you the thing you want.[100]

Es wird mir tatsächlich immer schwieriger, ja sinnloser, ein offizielles Englisch zu schreiben. Und immer mehr wie ein Schleier kommt mir meine Sprache vor, den man zerreissen muss, um an die dahinterliegenden Dinge (oder das dahinterliegende Nichts) zu kommen. Grammatik und Stil. Mir scheinen sie ebenso hinfällig geworden zu sein wie ein Biedermeier Badeanzug oder die Unerschütterlichkeit eines Gentlemans. [. . .] Ein Loch nach dem andern in ihr zu bohren, bis das Dahinterkauernde, sei es etwas oder nichts, durchzusickern anfängt – ich kann mir für den heutigen Schriftsteller kein höheres Ziel vorstellen.

It is indeed becoming more and more difficult, even senseless, for me to write an official English. And more and more my own language appears to me like a veil that must be torn apart in order to get at the things (or the Nothingness) behind it. Grammar and style. To me they seem to have become as irrelevant as a Victorian

45

bathing suit or the imperturbability of a true gentle-
man. [. . .] To bore one hole after another in it, until
what lurks behind it – be it something or nothing –
begins to seep through; I cannot imagine a higher goal
for a writer today.[101]

I come back to *faire* and *tout ça* (all that), *in French*
therefore.

Pas, you remember? No, not *Footfalls*, *Pas*. When
Pas says on p. 12: 'Dit comment c'était, tâche de dire
comment c'était. Tout ça.' (Beginning of the sixth
sequence.) 'Tout ça.' [102]

. . . 'IT CAN'T GO ON. . .' we think, and precisely it
goes on, one says it can't do what it's doing, and precisely
it does what it can't do. No. 'It can't go on', who says
that, this voice, you recognized it, did you not? it's Not
I, no, listen: '. . . it can't go on . . . all this [tout ça] . . .
all that [tout ça] . . . steady stream . . . straining to hear
. . . make something of it . . . and her own thoughts . . .
make something of them. . . all – [tout ça en][103] – you
recognize it? Not I. These words. And these dots [*points
de suspension*], which I am forced to name in bulk. In
order to distinguish them from the indication *a pause*,
for instance.

There are problems with each (non-)step, stop [*pas,
point*], deictic, etc. All this and that. All that but there's
never all, is there, *all that* is not *all*.

46

1.333333 is endless. There is a problem with division to infinity. Beckett or all the paradoxes of Zeno of Elea: dots do not make a straight line. It can't go on, it goes on.[104] Someone says *tout ça* in French. 'Dit comment c'était, tâche de dire comment c'était. Tout ça.' *Tout ça* a doubly mad phrase. This *all* which is *that*, has an intensifying value for that, but there may be not all that. That all adds up but to an absolutely indeterminate set. *Ça* (that, id): the thing, is the signature of the French language. *That's* just *that*. Nothing but that. The linguistic tag: what's *that*? A demonstrative. That is so true. A word that catches all, generalized phatic function. Extraordinary vicariousness, that is not all, that.

And who says: 'Tells how it all was'? May? or Amy? If it's May it's not Amy it's Amy otherwise. May, the signature in English. Is May Amy? Dismay![105] *Ça m'*. . .[106]

It's *Not I* who says that, it's Not-I. That is to say, the voice of (the) Mouth.

(The) Mouth, thus, the panting heroine of Not-I, the survivor, do you realize, the whole body being gone, by dint of struggling, straining to hear, nothing but mouth on fire. . . Dots. Words. Or Fire. . . Embers. . . On the subject of the Point or Dot. Dot. Dot. Dot: these are ghost letters. From very ancient times one has been used to saying in geometry: I take Point A and Point B. They are designated by letters. Takes a *name* to distinguish them. A sort of name. A or B. Their simplest expression.

The point is what doesn't have a word. Thus here is a text, a thing with words, which presents itself like a continuum words not words word not word, etc. Like I Not I I Not I Not. . . The Not I Series, summary sum(ma) time life God and all that. . . to resume from. Not I or Analysis.

Not aye

If I was asked to choose a text of Beckett's for all, for all that, I would certainly not do so but if I did, it would be *Not I*. Not why Not I? Why Not Not I? Analysis is the art of carving to infinity. The art of approaching, of Beckett the carver. While approaching the exact thing, thus first approximation and error, in order to correct the error you estimate the error by committing a smaller error, you approach the exact thing, the end, by making finer and finer errors. Variant: the alternate series. It's less great, it's less small or it's too great it's too small, correct, every other term by default, every other term by negative excess, whose model is Alice in Wonderland, there's a little lacking, there's a little too much, again, correct, approach, to resume, *still to be done*, he says. I would choose *Not I* arbitrarily. A passive decision. *Not I* chooses me. Poem, music, there's all that and the rest. What makes something be (not serial) *music*? (1) If you take a *totally random* series, there is nil correlation. No music.

(2) If you take a *totally correlated* series, you know exactly what's going to come. It's not music.

'1/f correlation' means that if you try to predict the following note, you have a fifty per cent chance of getting it wrong. The piece is sufficiently correlated for you to expect something, and yet for you to be *permanently surprised*. Bach's is the *perfect* 1/f correlated music. Bach. The perfect music of Not I *1/f correlated*. That is to say, structured *and* surprising. Sufficiently correlated for me to expect something (which is not always the case), for me to try to predict the following note but with a fifty per cent chance of getting it wrong. In order to be surprised, I must expect. And it does not happen. Not now. It can't go on. . . sudden longing to. . . re. . . tell. . . for a basin. . . then. . . to empty oneself in it [*s'y vider*]. . . so life [*si vie*] – *thrown up and back* [rendue].

Brilliant *Not I*, zero's neighbour, to die once or twice a year,[107] off text, in text, text off text me off me [*hors de moi*] in me, a twice slow race between stage and off stage. Everything takes place *after*. Imagine *after*. Curtain down. House back to dark. Then lighting from after, off stage, in text. A parergonal[108] spectacle, Jacques Derrida would say. *After* the curtain is fully down (italics, stage directions, belated stairs deductions [*didascalies, esprit de didescalier*][109]), one imagines the house, the people going out, thinking it's over, yet *the voice goes on the voice weakens* and ceases *as the house lights up*, the voice of

49

continuous darkness (says, does not say, the text, the not I, in italics), lit-up text, text in the dark.

> *Note*
> Movement: this consists in simple sideways raising of arms [. . .] in a gesture of reproach and helpless compassion. It lessens with each recurrence till scarcely perceptible at third. There is just enough pause to contain it as Mouth recovers from vehement refusal to relinquish third person.[110]

'Mouth' will have held on beyond the beyond. Held the not I it has won.[111] An unheard-of sentence which lets go of nothing. Resists. Not let go (of I). I never there. Prowls. Already heard Not I weaken. Weakening without end. Penultimate version of *Text for Nothing 13*. The weak old voice,[112] not I, refuses. The one that always says no. A paradoxical affirmation. Not aye: no. Not aye to life.

Sucer, s'user, re – what a story (untranslatable in English[113]). It takes so long to be done, the end never ends, is never done.

Malone needs Macmann in order to die in addition, one doesn't die, one is dying, one is dying oneself [*on se meurt*], one still stays [*on demeure encore*], one is still dying oneself again [*on se remeurt encore*], a little more still,

50

to keep using oneself up, to use usage, to use usury, to use using [*s'user à s'user, user d'usage, user d'usure, user d'usement*], to keep using oneself up in all senses and directions, all times and tenses, and mainly in the sense of collapsing, shattering to ground, of lowering with loss of breath, in successive crawlings and tumblings, to descend towards, also as a descent of previous descenders, as ancient verse and verse to come, to descend down a gentle slope whence[114] – no ascending back, only deadly stoppages [*arrêts de mort*],[115] that is to say, end stoppages, delays in dying, thus to die belatedly, in stages

What a story! But what does story mean?

Voice from *Cascando* dreams of ending it, that the story, that one, end, that Maunu[116] be done finally, but one can get towards the end only by disappointment, by relapses, must go back at it, more than once, each time this time *at last the right one*, and each time the right one, well no, it's not the right one, it's the rightnotone, what a story, it's the story of the story of the story which will end once, one day after the end, one has to go and die, there's somebody who serves as a messiah of death, he's got all it takes, a name with an M, Maunu, and a *manteau* (coat) with an M as well,

Voice, *Music*, dream of the time [*fois*], the right time, the last time, then sleeping, a dream of sleeping, but faith [*foi*] takes some begging, *this time* which would be the right time, every tenth year [*tous les dix ans*], every year,

51

and all those who say [*tous les disants*] that it would do well to come, what do they do, apart from praying, there are even cases when the whole life, all the time the whole act of living will have been nothing but reacting to the goad of time by getting out of the lifeless motionless sack of life [*sac à vivre*], halting, brooding, praying.

> Pause. The point draws back, pauses, darts forward into sack, withdraws, recoils to a foot short of sack. Pause. The sack does not move. The point draws back again, a little further than before, pauses, darts forward again into sack, withdraws, recoils to a foot short of sack. Pause. The sack moves. Exit goad.
> A crawls out of sack, halts, broods, prays.[117]

The end is the dream. Precisely the very last end, the final one, one goes there, one does nothing but go there, all of life in endless ever-ending [*finissance*], in progress, in the gerund, from falling [*chéance*] to falling, towards the promised deadline falling due [*échéance*], find what cannot be found, to be done with this self-befizzlement [*autoenfoirade*][118]

In the end to come to the end of the end, how to do that, it's hard, like the stone, it calls for a using up [*usement*] and a sucking up [*sucement*] more monstrously incessant than to drink the sea,[119] for at least, he says, even if it is horrifying to have to drink the sea, it allows one to think that at least there is the sea, but the end is not the sea to drink, that would be too much to hope for, that is to say, that would be impossible in reality but not in a dream, the end is to use up the unuseupable, and the stone of the unuseupable, Beckett will have spent all his life and afterwards the rest, sucking it for ten years then licking it ten years then turning it round and sucking it again on the other side and so on, sucking again what resists, the earth is full of holes, scratching the earth sucking the hole. *Sans*, pardon-less and pity-less. One must count up to this lessness[120] [*compter jusqu'à sans*], and tell up to a hundred [*raconter jusqu'à cent*], a hundred times the same story, since one must always rehash the same thing, do so just to store it [*histoire de*], what story? well, that, life, tell me your life, Sir. My life! – Well, yes, you know, this sort of – How should I put it? Now come on, everybody knows that. The main lines. Everybody's got some. Oh! how unspeakable life will have been, a sort of shadow. My shadow and [*et*] me, my shadow is [*est*] me.

Always the same thing which insists more and more urgently, implacably, always the same language that laps, the same jaw that gnaws at the speech a little more each day it chokes a little more with each sentence,

All that

There is no end, starting from a man who wants to end alone, says Jacques Derrida.[121]

Alone? But not without Not [*pas sans Pas*]. Not without Who, not without what and not without Voice.

Let's listen to *Cendres*, in French. In English, please note, *Embers*, not *Ashes*, not *Ash*, no, *Embers*, thus not 'Cendres', the French for 'Embers' would be *Braises*. But there you are, in the beginning *Embers*, 'Embers' was already the remains of 'Remembers'. Afterwards, then, Embers is reduced to *Cendres*.

Let's listen to *Embers*. Radioembers. This is Embers. Music of Embers. Embers of music. A stroke of genius: it is the sea, scarcely audible, which marks time, while my father, back from the dead, to be beside me, as if he had not died, makes not a sound, as if he had died.

BESIDE ME

Boots[122] *of Henry on shingle*. He halts. Steps Not [*Entre Pas*]. Not Henry [*Pas de Henry*]. I mean: Steps (not) of Henry [*Pas de Henry*]. Sound of step of Henry. Still audible rest of Henry. Step/Not. Who steps/not? [*Pas de qui?*] One does not know. On the radio it's the step of a Voice. One must wait half an hour for Ada, that is to say, the Voice Ada, *to name* the Voice that Steps. 'Laugh, Henry, it's not every day I crack a joke.' [123] Ah! now (No) Step hands over [*Pas passe la parole*] to Henry.

In the beginning No/Step of Henry, alone not alone,

54

alone but with Voice. The play takes the form of a fiction between Voices. Henry as voice that orders. Voice of the author, voice of God. Voice of Voice, Voice that calls other voices. One thinks, if one does, of Nietzsche's Last Philosopher as Jacques Derrida hears him, saying: *I am the last man.*[124] It is an unintelligible, untenable utterance but there is somebody to give it resonance, to listen to it, record it, publish it. It's Oedipus talking to himself, who is blind and whose voice is that of another. Oedipus dying as the last philosopher. Only one man alone dies. This long alas *Wehe Wehe* is the alas of the *Wehemensch*. Is it another, the man of alas, who dies outside me? It is as if Beckett was behind the page, recording this strange, twisted soliloquy.

> HENRY: On. [*Sea. Voice louder.*] On! [*He moves on. Boots on shingle. As he goes.*] Stop. [*Boots on shingle. As he goes, louder.*] Stop! [*He halts. Sea a little louder.*] Down. [*Sea. Voice louder.*] Down! [*Slither of shingle as he sits. Sea, still faint, audible throughout what follows whenever pause indicated.*] Who beside me now? [*Pause.*] An old man, blind and foolish. [*Pause.*] My father, back from the dead, to be with me [*Pause.*] As if he hadn't died. [*Pause.*] No, simply back from the dead, to be with me, in this strange place. [*Pause.*] Can he hear me? [*Pause.*] Yes, he must hear me. [*Pause.*] To answer me? [*Pause.*] No, he doesn't answer me. [*Pause.*] Just be with me.

[*Pause.*] That sound you hear is the sea. [*Pause. Louder.*] I say that sound you hear is the sea, we are sitting on the strand. [*Pause.*] I mention it because the sound is so strange, so unlike the sound of the sea, that if you didn't see what it was you wouldn't know what it was.[125]

Who beside me now? A subject without the verb to be. A nominal sentence. Who, without name, without noise, without being, in another room, would be another H, Hamlet.

The wave director or the omnipotent technician who authored *Embers* does, creates, discusses, wavers, moves forward backward, tries, just like God, it's not live, it's not definitive, if there's a smudge, one erases it, one goes backward, one resumes, one adjusts, just as God erases his first version of the world with a flood, and starts again. Dithers. Can he hear me? – Pause. – Yes, he must hear me. A little louder, a little less. He listens to his work and thinks it's no good. Afterthought. The sound of the sea not too great, so I say to the listener: it's the sea. There you are –

Mise en abyme of genesis. I, god, am saying on the microphone that that is the sea. Stronger than God: I am also God's witness, that is to say, I am myself and my own witness. That even beats it. On Thursday I say [*Le jeudi je dis*]: Hooves! Here I've just made a horse. Well, now we can start. What? The death struggle between

56

Father and son. To make a Father of oneself, in order to give oneself to be killed by the son one makes oneself to be. It is better than the Shakespeare in *Ulysses*,[126] and it's live. Performative. Thus to double Hamlet, to do Oedipus and his solitude, to set the *Letter to the Father* to waves as a Father, Hermann, and son, Franz,[127] to hand over the ventriloquist microphone to all the fighters, at will, but not automatically. The Sound Engineer has to deal with other willpowers than his own, the stage is in his belly and outside, the Horse needs begging, all is not equally given, the listener is held breathless, in front of the improvised act of the mental tightrope walker. One pricks up one's ears. Where are we? At the mental theatre, at the circus, in the head of the World Improviser, without any facility. What a pity! What a pity one cannot be alone. One is dependent on one's head, on the paternal genitor, one's got to do it all, do the head, do the father so he does somebody to whom one can speak, to do in [*se faire*] the father, or anybody, the first come who will be able to recognize the (f)actor[128] and thus act or do the father, a bit of father for him, enough to make an act, from there to carry on within the father in order to derive Ada, Ada, what a find. Where did he get that one from? Made to measure. She does what she can, and he makes her do everything she can and everything he can. 'Precious little'.[129] He, Beckett, invented auto-affective radiotelephony. Graft-phony. He does voices to himself.

57

And he trains them the way Chaplin trains imaginary fleas.[130] Hop! This calls for a juggler's agility and attention. For it all happens on the rays and spokes [*rayons*] of the void. In the cup, head, basin

Facing the end like the man from the country before the law, *vor dem Gesetz*[131] poor beggar who already tried in vain, in Kafka's time, to go through, already begged, all his life, the doorkeeper to let him enter the Law, *in das Gesetz, but now is not the time*, and who comes back under the name of Malone, or A, or Hamm, or Voice, to present himself again before (the law) the promised peace

End of which, face in the mud, face in the sand head in the sack, the voice in the head, one can have a foretaste, vaguely, a vaguetaste, of nothing more, that's it, says the sentence which precedes and interrupts, well, not yet, a crawling sisyphism.[132] Ditto for *how it is*

How It Is is a flow of paragraphs, a flow disconcerted by all sorts of speaking persons, a cacophony, each syntactical fragment which interrupts the other is a broken sentence. There are *insistences*: the question of memory, pseudo-biographical questioning, there is a form: polylogue, amphipolylogical:

'– do you love me *cunt* [con]?'

It's amphibological – cunt? cunt – stantly

'– the same too [*la même chan*]. . .'

discourse passes over now under silence now above it.

58

It *looks* [l'air] like it's obeying the *con* – vention of the paragraph, but it *sounds* a different toon [chan – *son*][133]

How is it that they start, these paragraphs?[134] It does not start. It is started. It is how it is [*C'est commencé. C'est comment c'est*].

How It Is is always already to start again from the first thinking breath to the last, ditto every sixth line, with a difference, what a difference, in this case the word *yes* alternates with the word *no*, which changes nothing in the situation, if he likes to sing no but sometimes he does yes always the same tune for some time yes, the same time no, no word being able to have the last word or claiming to be the last word,

> [. . .] until at last good he wins life here this life he can't

> questions then DO YOU LOVE ME CUNT that family cut thrust to make an end got there at last if he remembers how he got here no one day he found himself here yes like when one is born yes manner of speaking yes if he knows how long ago no not even a rough idea no if he remembers how he lived no always lived like that yes flat on his belly in the mud yes in the dark yes with his sack yes

> [. . .] never a gleam no never a soul no never a voice no I the first yes never stirred no crawled no a few yards no

59

ate pause ATE good and deep no if he knows what's in
the sack no never had the curiosity no if he thinks he
can die one day pause DIE ONE DAY no

[. . .] if he talks to himself no thinks no believes in God
yes every day no wishes to die yes but doesn't expect to
no he expects to stay where he is flat as a cowclap on his
belly yes in the mud yes without motion yes without
thought yes eternally yes[135]

Not only you shall not kill, no, the curse is *you shall
not die* you shall expect nothing but that you shall expect
That, this That which, with every step you creep and
crawl towards it, manages to still keep at the same distance, you didn't expect that, in the faraway time when
you were put to sand, to ground, in this vicious world,
a larva in the cylinder, you entered and enter again each
time already interned in the logomotive, churned about,
but if That still remains not seen not visible not so absolutely invisible, not that near not that far, it's because
you cannot do otherwise, physically, instinctually, than
to seek outside what is inside yourself, you get bits of
thought and scraps of speech unstuck which you edge
forward towards That-before-you, whereas That and you
are undissociated, indissociable. Between you and That,
in other words the event of dying to which you address
the whole of your being in remains, there is nothing but

60

the membrane of torment. *That* will never happen in your time, all your efforts printed under tattered paper covers, the dreamed time of a book, will be brutally scattered-erased by a dash, a spotlight that goes off, the invasion of a silence, of a sea, of a non-response, of an absence, of an infinite withdrawal – of what Kafka would call Help, the one that does not come, and that you do not call for at all, does not happen, no name, no. *That* will happen but not to you, that will happen only one day after you. Will come one day after you, and sweep away.

    – No literature!
    – Less and less literature
    – Less and less words
    – – and –
    – –

Beckett the sweeper: he sweeps words away from his own texts and he needs ten years per page, to sweep *Texts for Nothing 13* till *Not I* 1950 till 1973 twenty-three years he needs to sweep away remains of I from Old Voice till Mouth. . . etc.

Beckett the emaciator. To emaciate language. Down to skin, film [*pellicule*], down to *Film*.

Swept away. Are we inside? Are we outside? All that is at the Theatre. It's all theatre. Which can't go on unless at the Theatre. At the Not (of the) Theatre.

Now imagine the Great One the one who intimates the order: *imagine*. The one, the first, who said to the audience: imagine! Just figure!

> [. . .] Suppose that you have seen
> The well-appointed king at Dover pier
> Embark his royalty, and his brave fleet
> With silken streamers the young Phoebus fanning.
> [. . .]
> Now entertain conjecture of a time
> When creeping murmur and the poring dark
> Fills the wide vessel of the universe.
> From camp to camp through the foul womb of night
> The hum of either army stilly sounds,
> That the fixed sentinels almost receive
> The secret whispers of each other's watch.
> Fire answers fire, and through their paly flames
> Each battle sees the other's umbered face.[136]

It's Shakespeare, he can't be seen, he's sitting in a corner of the room, he's paring his fingernails, as Joyce says,[137] and he is *prompting*. He does the characters. And he does the audience. The whole world within, without, stage left stage right, is prompted, everything is dictated. The author, or prompter, or dictator is the omnipotent

62

conjurer. One sometimes may succumb to his spells. And then on p. 73 or p. 173 he gets up and throws us out the cardboard door.

No matter how silent, how engrossed in paring his fingernails, how plunged in absence, it seems he will have thought only about leading us on.

One knows the old bond [*liaison*] between psychoanalysis and the theatre, the *old* bond, says Jacques Derrida, with Belacqua's Beckettian accent:

> Will it always be the same theatrical structure? Will it still be tomorrow, in the next millennium, the same model, the same apparatus, the same theatrical family? Will it be the same theater of the same family, an always more or less royal family, rather patriarchal and heterosexual, installed in sexual difference as binary opposition?[138]

Between analysis, unbinding,[139] and the thin invisible layerless cylinder which contains the unbound between the staging of the subject in pieces [*mise en pièces du sujet*] and the theatre. Between the scene and the Not-I family.

The Theatre-Head, the Theatre beneath the skull, the Theatre of Being and *the being-perceived*, therefore *the theatred being* in person, Beckett's Head. The Theatre has always been waiting for Beckett, as the Whale is waiting for Jonah,[140] and afterwards, when Jonah comes out of the theatre of the Whale he just has to let the head of the audience imagine the Whale. One comes out of a Theatre to find oneself in another Theatre, one is a foetus in a rosy theatre, one is born in a verdure, azure,[141] sea, etc. theatre, not only, one is made to do theatre to be and to make stage. *To make stage, not sense*. Beckett not philosopher, no, a man for the theatre, a theatre-man. To make stage with all means and me's available [*de tout bois de tout moi*], to dim the limelights till *Embers*. To decimate *the big original sham* and to decimate *the small sham specially destined to each case*, to calm right down to the dead calm. Agitation Beckett calmed on 22 December 1989. Last cliché and snapshot: he is resting. No, he has travelled. Is no longer [*en train*]. . . – asking – where now. Lost consciousness. He did say: when I lose consciousness it will not be to recover it.[142] At last without witness. Forever 'signifying nothing'.[143]

FOR A FINAL ATTEMPT TO BE DONE WITH ENDING IN BODY AND SOUL WITH BECKETT

Dream dated 8 September 2006

It's an ordeal for me and for the others. Two hours have already passed and I still haven't managed to undress. Yet I'm doing nothing but that. It must be said that I'm much overdressed even more than I knew myself, for I've forgotten since this morning. It was cold at dawn. To my credit I wanted to go out for some air, to sit outside at a table, alone, in front of my papers. At that moment I was ahead of the world. I was fresh. Then the people came, the friends too, including the pensioner from the National Rail Company and Sorbonne his wife. At that moment the time came for me to catch up on the time of others. The thing is, though up so early, I hadn't had a wash. Therefore I asked my visitors to wait for a moment, to give me time to have a shower. The shower's right here, two metres away. I'm quick. That'll only take a minute. I get the bathrobe and the towel ready. True it's open, perhaps people will see me but this is not my concern. On the one hand it goes very fast, the water hides your body, then there's the bathrobe, I say to myself, too bad if people see me it's no big deal I have nice curves, nothing dishonourable. However, I'm not there yet, far from it. I must still get to the end of the undressing. I first took off a pullover with some difficulty. This is due to the fact that I put it on over another, hence how cramped it felt. There's also something which resists in the pullover, which just won't come off. Ditto for the bottom part. The trousers. Under the trousers I discover I have tights. Alas tights are tight. It takes me an age to wrench them away. A good quarter of an hour. Meanwhile I keep my visitors company, I talk to them. I tell them what I heard at the last lecture and which might interest them. These tights finally come off only to make me discover I have socks. Oh I had put on socks last night alas. They cling well. I finally manage to get rid of them after a quarter of an hour. I look at the shower. Another quarter of an hour. The T-shirt kills me – it's a struggle, the arms cling to my arms, how to wrench my arms away from these arms and besides with which arms? I contort myself, it exhausts me, when I'm finally done, I'm worn out, I no longer have arms and naturally what do I see another T-shirt, the last one but I have no strength and arms left. It's the old farce: we hold the world and we complain that it holds us. I turn towards Sorbonne. Sorbonne, what a name! If you could help me and pull at the sleeves? Disapprovingly she begrudges some help. Whereas I need a force equivalent to the force of resistance. . . Pull! Pull! I implore. I only think of

the time when I'm finally undressed. When I have a shower.
But it's a dream. For the moment I still have a T-shirt the
bra, and no more strength at all except anguish. And the
quick shower still waiting. Or else have a shower with this
last underwear? No. But soon. Let's resume. Two hours.
How to apologize? Now the floor around me is strewn with a
huge pile of clothes, all that. . . It seems to me the end is near.
I'm getting there. I can already see myself turning on the tap.
Oh! The cap. Yes, that's so simple, this is why I'd not even
noticed it. Surely it won't resist me, will it? No. I'm located
under the showerhead. In a few moments I am going (1) to
whisk off my cap (2) to quickly turn on the tap. That'll have
taken me two hours and two minutes. I can see the end. I'm
worn out, I'm worn out. Curtain.

1 Part of Macbeth's famous tirade following the news of Lady Macbeth's death in Shakespeare's eponymous play (*Macbeth*, Act III, sc. v, l. 23); see n. 143 below. The next two quoted fragments, also in the original in Cixous's text, are ll. 20 and 21 in the play. – Trans.

2 '*un* peux *précieux*', a near-homophone of the literal translation in French of Beckett's 'precious little': *peu précieux* (see also pp. 4, 9, 57 below. – Trans.

3 See Molloy's words: 'I listen and the voice is of a world collapsing endlessly, a frozen world.' Samuel Beckett, *Molloy*, in *The Beckett Trilogy* (London: Pan Books, 1979), p. 38. See also p. 24 below. – Trans.

4 Originally a character in Dante's *Purgatory*, canto IV symbolizing sloth and negligence, Belacqua is one of Beckett's first *personae* to have made its fictional mark, from his first novel *Dream of Fair to Middling Women* (1932) onwards (see p. 43 below), including in the short story 'Dante and the Lobster'. – Trans.

5 '*clopant-clopé*' punningly combines *clopin-clopant*: hobbling along, and *éclopé*: limping, lame. – Trans.

6 The word is in English in the text. – Trans.

7 Shem and Shaun are the twin brothers in James Joyce's *Finnegans Wake*, for which Beckett served as an amanuensis in the late 1920s. In Part I, chapter 7 of Joyce's novel, the answer to the 'first riddle of the universe', 'when is a man not a man?', is 'when he is a [. . .] Sham';

James Joyce, *Finnegans Wake* (London: Faber, 1975), p. 170. – Trans.

8 An allusion to Beckett's seminal essay on *Finnegans Wake*, 'Dante. . . Bruno. Vico. . Joyce' – thus punctuated as an allusion to Vico's three cycles of his Ideal Eternal History used as a structural prop in Joyce's novel – originally published in a co-edited collection known as *Our Exagmination Round His Factification for Incamination of 'Work in Progress'* (London: Faber and Faber, 1929). See nn. 26 and 57 below. – Trans.

9 German *grausam*: terrible, and *grau*: grey. – Trans.

10 A double allusion to Jacques Derrida's 'Two Words for Joyce' (on *Finnegans Wake*) and his elliptical definition of deconstruction as '*plus d'une langue*' in *Memoires for Paul de Man*, rev. edn, trans. Cecile Lindsay *et al.* (New York: Columbia University Press, 1986), p. 15. – Trans.

11 A compact allusion to the skull in the guise of a white rotunda in Beckett's 'Imagination Dead Imagine', trans. by the author, in *Samuel Beckett: The Complete Short Prose, 1929–1989*, ed., intro. and notes by S. E. Gontarski (New York: Grove Press, 1995), pp. 182–5. – Trans.

12 For instance, Freud mentions an 'instinct of cruelty' – or, for Jacques Derrida in 'Psychoanalysis Searches the States of Its Soul' (see n. 138 below), a 'cruelty drive' – in his *Three Essays on the Theory of Sexuality*. – Trans.

13 From *cruor*: shed blood, also used in this etymological vein by Jacques Derrida in 'Circumfession', trans. Geoffrey Bennington, in Geoffrey Bennington and Jacques Derrida, *Jacques Derrida* (Chicago and London: University of Chicago Press, 1993), period 1, pp. 7–8. – Trans.

14 '*Paris, tenu*', also a pun on *pari tenu*, a phrase uttered

69

when one has managed to pull off (lit.: hold) something one said one would (see also n. 111 below). The idiom is then made to connect forward with Dante and Mandelstam via '*tenu*': held. – Trans.

15 This may refer more specifically to Estragon, one of the four main characters in Beckett's play *Waiting for Godot*, often featured sitting on a mound in a foetal posture. – Trans.

16 This description is borrowed from Beckett's study of Marcel Proust; see Samuel Beckett, *Proust and Three Dialogues with Georges Duthuit* (London: John Calder, 1965), p. 35. – Trans.

17 See n. 22 below. – Trans.

18 The title of Beckett's only published collection of poems (1935) as well as a title piece. – Trans.

19 'I think that life would suddenly seem wonderful to us if we were threatened to die as you say. Just think of how many projects, travels, love affairs, studies, it – our life – holds in dissolution, invisible to our laziness which, certain of the future, postpones them incessantly.

But let all this threaten to become impossible for ever, how beautiful it will become again! Ah! If only the cataclysm doesn't take place this time, we won't miss visiting the new galleries of the Louvre, throwing ourselves at the feet of Miss X [. . .], making a trip to India. The cataclysm doesn't take place, we don't do any of it, for we find ourselves back in the heart of normal life, where negligence blunts desire.

And yet we shouldn't have needed the cataclysm to love life today. It would have been enough to think that we are humans, and that death may come this evening.' (Marcel Proust, in *Contre Sainte-Beuve* (Paris: Gallimard, 1971), pp. 645–6 [trans. Laurent Milesi].)

20 This and the next two quotations are in English in the text. – Trans.

21 Beckett, shortly before his death, thirteen days precisely, to his friend John Montague, who comes and pays him a visit in the clinic of the 14th arrondissement in Paris. Last interview, 'A Few Drinks and a Hymn: My Farewell to Samuel Beckett', reported in the *New York Times*, 17 April 1994. I am grateful to my friend Elissa Marder for the recall of this recall. [This was followed in the original by Cixous's French translation, omitted here. – Trans.]

22 Like the cup of lime tea in which the famous *madeleine* is dunked, the uneven cobble in the courtyard of the Guermantes Hotel and in Saint Mark's Baptistry in Venice, the noise of the spoon on the plate, the starched rigidity of the napkin, and the hissing sound of the water in the pipes are examples of Proustean anamnesis or involuntary memory in *À la recherche du temps perdu* (*In Search of Lost Time*). Together with George Sand's novel *François le Champi*, these are Proust's 'last five visitations' according to Beckett himself in his *Proust*, p. 38. – Trans.

23 Samuel Beckett, '. . . but the clouds. . . A play for television', in *The Complete Dramatic Works* (London: Faber, 1986), p. 420.

24 See Dante Alighieri, *Purgatory*, canto XV.

25 The fragments in italics are borrowed from Beckett's *Proust*, p. 15. – Trans.

26 This sequence, especially the italics, is a collage from the end of *Company*, whose last, detached word is 'Alone'; see *Samuel Beckett. The Grove Centenary Edition. Volume IV: Poems, Short Fiction, Criticism*, series ed. Paul Auster, intro. J. M. Coetzee (New York: Grove Press, 2006), p. 450. In the context of the following paragraph, one may

also suspect a reference to the famous Paris literary book-shop Shakespeare and Company, which helped publish Joyce's *Ulysses* as well as its French translation and the collection *Our Exagmination Round His Factification for Incamination of Work in Progress*, both in 1929. – Trans.

27   Samuel Beckett, 'The Lost Ones', trans. by the author, in *The Complete Short Prose*, p. 223. [Compare with a similar extract on zero temperature in a contemporaneous piece, 'Imagination Dead Imagine' (*The Complete Short Prose*, pp. 182–3). The French title for 'The Lost Ones', *Le Dépeupleur* (Paris: Minuit, 1970), has been rendered more literally in Cixous's text to allow for a smoother integration of her use of its semantic associations (*dépeupler*: to deplete, depopulate). – Trans.]

28   Derrida identified with the figure of the Jewish Marrano in several texts of the 1990s, starting with 'Circumfession', where he also writes of himself as *le dernier des Juifs*: the last (and least) of the Jews (period 36, p. 190). – Trans.

29   Primo Levi's famous autobiographical account of survival in Auschwitz, *Se questo è un uomo* (1947), translated as *If This Is a Man*, featuring the opposite characters of Elias Lindzin and 'Null Achtzehn' (naught eighteen, the last three digits of his prisoner's number), the archetypes of the scheming survivor and the damned in the German *Lager* (camp) respectively. – Trans.

30   Respectively the deformed hunchback in Victor Hugo's novel *Notre Dame de Paris* and the savage in Shakespeare's *The Tempest*. – Trans.

31   The title of one of the three novels of Beckett's Trilogy, with *Molloy* and *Malone Dies*. – Trans.

32   '*Longtemps*' happens to be the first word of the famous beginning of Proust's *À la recherche du temps perdu*: '*Longtemps, je me suis couché de bonne heure*'. – Trans.

33 In English in the text. – Trans.

34 In English in the text. An echo of Prospero's 'the isle is full of noises' in *The Tempest*, Act III, sc. 2, l. 147, but also Cixous's own variation, 'The island is full of voices. The time is full of questions. Around you-Proteus-Prospero, questions arise all the time', already performed in 'Jacques Derrida as a Proteus Unbound', *Critical Inquiry*, vol. 33, no. 2: 'The Late Derrida', ed. W. J. T. Mitchell and Arnold I. Davidson (Winter 2007), p. 393. – Trans.

35 The beginning of Beckett's 'Imagination Dead Imagine', in *The Complete Short Prose*, p. 182. – Trans.

36 An allusion to Pascal's description of man as a 'thinking reed' (*roseau pensant*) in his *Pensées*, which the omnipresence of hats as a symbol of human essence and existence in Beckett's works may be seen to debunk. – Trans.

37 Samuel Beckett, 'Fizzle 4', trans. by the author, *Fizzles*, in *The Complete Short Prose*, p. 234.

38 '*Pitrerie. Petrerie. Tous les pets de travers*', involving puns on French *contrepet* (literally: counterfart) or *contrepeterie*: spoonerism. A *pet de travers*, literally 'fart the wrong way', is also used to refer to blunders, hence the double gaffe and guff (also in the slang sense of a puff of bad wind) in the translation to further echo the meaning of Beckett's *Fizzles* or, in French, *Foirades* (with *foirer*: to fizzle out). – Trans.

39 In the original this passage 'stages' the wearing thin of language one work after another by stripping letters off *bordure*, then *ordure*, then *-dure* (*durer*: to last). – Trans.

40 The title of the last poem Beckett wrote in French, which he then translated into English as 'What is the Word'. – Trans.

41 The English and French titles of Samuel Beckett's penultimate prose piece. – Trans.

42 '*Sans point. Sans pas. Sans. Tiens, voilà que ça fait passant!*': I have tried to adapt the punning homophony and the play on negatives (*sans, pas* – for these, see also below – *point*) in the French. – Trans.

43 Plays on *putain de vie*: bloody (lit.: whore of a) life. – Trans.

44 Beckett, *Waiting for Godot*, in *The Complete Dramatic Works*, p. 44; *En attendant Godot* (Paris: Minuit, 1952), p. 79. [Cixous quotes both versions, which are therefore given in reverse order. – Trans.]

45 A portmanteau word (chaos + cosmos) that appears in James Joyce's *Finnegans Wake*, p. 118. – Trans.

46 This Irishization of 'Eye', not irrelevant in a context discussing both Joyce's and Beckett's eyesight, has been resorted to in order to keep the visual emphasis on the Object and Obstacle O throughout as well as distance the aural impact of the English word, which homophonically sounds the same as the letter 'I'. – Trans.

47 Milton's dramatic play *Samson Agonistes* starts *in medias res*, with Samson, a prisoner to the Philistines, having had his eyes cut out (see l. 66: 'Blind among enemies, O worse than chains'). – Trans.

48 James Joyce suffered several attacks of glaucoma, especially during the time of his acquaintance with Beckett in Paris in the 1920s. – Trans.

49 Coined from Jacques Derrida's notion of the *faux-bond*, as in, for example, '*Ja*, or the *faux-bond* II ', in *Points. . . Interviews, 1974–1994*, ed. Elisabeth Weber, trans. Peggy Kamuf et al. (Stanford: Stanford University Press, 1995), pp. 30–77. In French *faire faux bond* means 'to let [somebody] down'. – Trans.

50 Dante Alighieri, *Purgatory*, canto IV, l. 43 (trans. Laurent Milesi).

51 The French *'normal. Normante'* can also be heard as a recall of the one-time advertising catchphrase for Normandy butter: *'c'est normal, c'est normand'*, which would thus anticipate the sequence on margarine below. – Trans.

52 What follows is a running paraphrase of the verse preceding *Purgatory*, canto IV, l. 43. – Trans.

53 An allusion to the French idiom in the subtitle of Derrida's 'Un Ver à soie. Points de vue piqués sur l'autre voile', in Hélène Cixous and Jacques Derrida, *Voiles* (Paris: Galilée, 1998), pp. 23–85, where *piquer* means both 'to steal' in colloquial French (to nick) and 'to stitch'. – Trans.

54 Respectively a locality in the Italian region Marche where Dante stayed and a geological formation in north-central Italy climbed by the Italian poet; see Dante Alighieri, *Purgatory*, canto IV, ll. 25–30. – Trans.

55 Dante Alighieri, *Purgatory*, canto IV, l. 46. – Trans.

56 This and the following development 'writes through' Beckett's short prose text 'Imagination Dead Imagine' (*The Complete Short Prose*, pp. 182-85). – Trans.

57 Samuel Beckett, 'Dante. . . Bruno. Vico. . Joyce', in *Disjecta. Miscellaneous Writings and a Dramatic Fragment*, ed. and foreword by Ruby Cohn (London: John Calder, 1983), p. 33. [The quotation was followed by Cixous's own French translation, omitted here. – Trans.]

58 The formula is used at the beginning of 'Ding-Dong', in Samuel Beckett, *More Pricks than Kicks* (London: Calder and Boyars, 1966), p. 39. – Trans.

59 The last two phrases occur in 'Ding-Dong', in *More Pricks than Kicks*, p. 39. – Trans.

60 Dante Alighieri, *Purgatory*, canto IV, ll. 103-114. [Here I have used Laurence Binyon's rhymed translation

published in *The Portable Dante*, ed. and intro. Paolo Milano (Harmondsworth: Penguin, 1947). – Trans.]

61 Gilles Deleuze, 'The Exhausted', in *Essays Critical and Clinical*, trans. Daniel W. Smith and Michael A. Greco (London and New York: Verso, 1998), p. 163 (translation slightly modified by Laurent Milesi).

62 First given in its French translation (*Hue!*), then quoted in English in the text. – Trans.

63 A well-respected French academic and supervisor of Cixous's *thèse d'état* on Joyce. A personal friend of Beckett, on whom he published several essays, he made possible Cixous's meeting with the Irish writer alluded to on p. 18. – Trans.

64 Beckett, *Waiting for Godot*, in *The Complete Dramatic Works*, p. 39. [Only the last cue is to be found in the English version. – Trans.]

65 Beckett, *Waiting for Godot*, in *The Complete Dramatic Works*, pp. 28–9 (author's emphasis).

66 The thirteenth of Franz Kafka's 'Meditations on Sin, Suffering, Hope and the True Path', posthumously published by Max Brod in 1931 (trans. from the original by Laurent Milesi).

67 Beckett, *Worstward Ho*, in *The Grove Centenary Edition. Volume IV*, p. 479. [This passage also concludes Deleuze's essay 'The Exhausted' (see n. 61 above). – Trans.]

68 An allusion to Kafka's short story 'The Great Wall of China'. – Trans.

69 Beckett, *Embers. A Piece for Radio*, in *The Complete Dramatic Works*, p. 254.

70 This cross between French *quoi*, what, suggestive of pedantic interrogation, and a duck's quacking occurs repeatedly in *How It Is*. Its antecedent may be the equally dismissive 'quaquaquaqua', itself possibly influenced by

a more convoluted but similar nonce-word in Joyce's *Finnegans Wake* (p. 195), in Lucky's sudden outpouring towards the end of Act I in *Waiting for Godot* (*The Complete Dramatic Works*, p. 40). – Trans.

71 In French *Ouf*, which, here and elsewhere, plays on the interjection but also on French back slang (*verlan*) for *fou*: mad, like *faire œuf* (lit.: to make egg) for *faire feu*: to open fire. Up to the end of this paragraph the translation will 'swap' the two languages in order to render the performative dimension of Cixous's text at this point, hence the original '*Rien qu'en français*', in French, becoming 'Just in English' in English (see 'In-traduction'). – Trans.

72 Beckett, *Embers*, in *The Complete Dramatic Works*, p. 261.

73 This Latin saying means 'through hardships to the stars' and is also obviously intended as a pun on the French brand of margarine, *Astra* (BlueBand), mentioned before. See *Embers*, in *The Complete Dramatic Works*, p. 256. – Trans.

74 An allusion to a famous sentence in Edgar Quinet's *Introduction à la philosophie de l'histoire de l'humanité* about the passing of time and the recurrence of historical cycles, used by Joyce as a leitmotif in *Finnegans Wake*, especially p. 281. – Trans.

75 A possible further reference to the passing of time as it expressed repeatedly in *Finnegans Wake* via Vico's eternal cycles and formula combining past, present and future. – Trans.

76 *Pas un chat*: idiomatically, not a living soul (see *Embers*, in *The Complete Dramatic Works*, p. 261), adapted here in order to translate what follows – Trans.

77 Those four characters appear in the plays *Eh Joe*, *Happy Days*, *Endgame*, and *Krapp's Last Tape* respectively. – Trans.

78 Beckett, *Embers*, in *The Complete Dramatic Works*, p. 261 (translation slightly amended to reflect Cixous's text later on).

79 '*Faire image, faire murmure, faire fi, faire f.*' See p. 33 and n. 71 above about the translation of *faire œuf, faire feu, faire ouf*, and the performative reversal of 'phew' into *ouf*; *faire fi* means 'to flout'. Making or doing the image – see the end of 'The Image', trans. Edith Fournier, in *The Complete Short Prose*, p. 168, and also p. 18 above – in Beckett's texts is discussed extensively in Deleuze's 'The Exhausted'. – Trans.

80 An allusion to the famous line by Molière's character in his play *Le Bourgeois Gentilhomme*, after being informed that there is no other way of expressing oneself than prose or verse, that for forty years he had been speaking prose without knowing it. – Trans.

81 'Nothing but' and 'no butt' attempt to render the play in '*rien que tête sans queue, tête à queue, rien que*' (*faire un tête-à-queue* [for a car]: to spin round, lit.: to do a head to tail). This passage weaves in elements from Beckett's play *Happy Days*: Winnie's capacious bag which stores her life's paraphernalia, the handkerchief, the adjective 'old', etc. – Trans.

82 Here Cixous's text, as in the following quotation (including the first square-bracketed addition) and explanation, plays on the discrepancy between the French stage direction *temps*: time(s), and its English equivalent, pause. – Trans.

83 Beckett, *Happy Days*, in *The Complete Dramatic Works*, pp. 158–9. [Cixous's footnote further explains that she emphasizes the homophony between *temps* and *t'en* in French, which is lost in the English version. – Trans.]

84 This refers to Hamlet's celebrated reply to Rosencrantz

and Guildenstern in *Hamlet*, Act II, sc. ii, ll. 264–5.
– Trans.

85 Beckett's own translation of the French version, titled *Bing* – hence Cixous's play on 'being' – was *Ping*. – Trans.

86 The French 'SANS MOT DIRE' can be read as *Sans*, Beckett's French original, which he translated as *Lessness*; *sans mot*: wordless; *dire*: say; but also perhaps the homophone *maudire*, pronounced like *mot dire*: to curse. – Trans.

87 There follows a long development playing across the two languages involving *dis*, *faire* and *diffère* – similar in homophonic effect and semantic discrepancy to 'gain', 'say' and 'gainsay' – and, again, *f eff*ects in French and English as F and E (see 'In-traduction'). – Trans.

88 '*bien entendu*': of course, but also, more literally and appropriately in the context of homophonic play, well heard. – Trans.

89 Added to the text in order to keep the performative dimension of the original address 'in French' in an English translation, in a context emphasizing the issue of (in)fidelity in language, hence the deliberate Gallicisms in this section (see 'In-traduction'). – Trans.

90 There may be an added allusion to the sequence in *Embers* when Addie, practising a piece by Chopin, plays an E instead of an F, and her music master violently exclaims 'Eff! Eff!' repeatedly (*The Complete Dramatic Works*, pp. 258–9). – Trans.

91 A hilarious portmanteau joke in the original on *bénéfice*: benefit, and *ben et fils*: Arabic and French for 'son', in a phrase suggestive of a family business. – Trans.

92 *Pas*: at once the French negation (not) and the word for 'step', as in Maurice Blanchot's *Le Pas au-delà*, translated as *The Step Not Beyond*. All the *pas* in Cixous's text,

starting with the inaugural 'step' on p. 1, could be re-read and heard in this *double entendre*. – Trans.

93 In fact the *OED* records two senses for 'pas': the right of going first, precedence (in several now obsolete set phrases); and dancing steps. Later on, Beckett's short play *Pas*, self-translated as *Footfalls*, is discussed. – Trans.

94 The sequence is obviously in English in the original. – Trans.

95 '*sans sans, sans sang sans cent nom de sans*'. I have supplied English equivalents to the French homophones based on Beckett's own choice of '-less' in his own translation (see n. 86 above). '*nom de sans*' can be understood as a swearing formula, as in 'by X'. – Trans.

96 Jaques's famous words in Shakespeare's play *As You Like It*, Act II, sc. vii, l.166. – Trans.

97 Literally: lanky, but our priority has been to keep the 'eff' alliteration (see 'In-traduction'). – Trans.

98 '*fait maigre*' also means 'not to eat meat', hence the added reference to fasting further down. – Trans.

99 A reference to Rimbaud's celebrated *lettre du Voyant*, written to Paul Demeny on 15 May 1871, in which he famously asserted that 'I is an other'. – Trans.

100 Extract from *Dream of Fair to Middling Women*, in Samuel Beckett, *Disjecta*, p. 47. [The quotation was followed by Cixous's own French translation, omitted here. – Trans.]

101 Beckett's German Letter to Axel Kaun, dated 9 July 1937, in *Disjecta*, p. 52, trans. Martin Esslin on pp. 171–2.

102 'Tells how it was. [. . .] Tries to tell how it was. [. . .] It all.' *Footfalls*, in *The Complete Dramatic Works*, p. 401. The following passages play on the all-purpose *ça* in French and I have tried to keep a recognizable, yet

consistent set of minimal translation choices for Cixous's barrage of resistingly idiomatic phrases. – Trans.

103   Beckett, *Not I*, in *The Complete Dramatic Works*, p. 380. – Trans.

104   Apart from the allusion to *Not I* seen above, see the ending of *The Unnamable*: 'I can't go on, I'll go on' (*The Beckett Trilogy*, p. 382). – Trans.

105   Both in English in the original. May is one of the two characters of *Footfalls*, who anagrammatically turns into Amy. – Trans.

106   The truncated form of 'it + verb + me' in French, possibly suggestive of suppressed annoyance (*ça m'. . .énerve*), also sounding like 'Sam'. – Trans.

107   Here and throughout this sequence, Cixous performs freely correlated variations on the words and stage directions of *Not I*. – Trans.

108   Derrida first developed his notion of the *parergon* (frame; lit.: outside the work – *hors oeuvre*), borrowed from Kant's *Critique of Judgement*, in *The Truth in Painting*, trans. Geoff Bennington and Ian McLeod (Chicago: Chicago University Press, 1987). – Trans.

109   A compact pun involving the French idiom *avoir l'esprit d'escalier*, used when one thinks of a perfect answer too late, here applied to spectators leaving the theatre thinking the play is over and realizing belatedly on the stairs that the voice of 'Not I' was still speaking. – Trans.

110   Beckett, *Not I*, in *The Complete Dramatic Works*, p. 375 (text slightly amended in order to keep closer to the French).

111   '*Tenu le pas moi gagné*': one can think of *pari tenu, gagné*, said about a bet taken up and won. – Trans.

112   See Beckett, 'Texts for Nothing 13', trans. by the author, in *The Complete Short Prose*, p. 152. – Trans.

113 The 'untranslatable' title of this section can be given literally as: To suck, to use oneself up, re, with perhaps *resucée*: rehash (and, more literally, sucking again, what Beckett's characters, especially Molloy, keep doing with stones). – Trans.

114 '*descendre en pente d'où*', in which one may also hear the beginning of *en pente douce*: gently sloping, hence the addition of 'gentle' to the translation. – Trans.

115 The phrase can be understood either as the legal idiom meaning a death sentence or, more literally, especially since Derrida's reading of Maurice Blanchot's similarly titled novel – see 'Living On: Borderlines', in *Deconstruction and Criticism*, ed. Geoffrey Hartman et al. (London: Routledge and Kegan Paul, 1979), pp. 75–176 – as what puts an end to death, hence the translation. – Trans.

116 The character in the French original of Beckett's play *Cascando*, subtitled 'A radio play for music and voice', whose name may be parsed as 'naked miseries' (*maux nus*), was changed to Woburn in the English version. – Trans.

117 Beckett, *Act Without Words II*, in *The Complete Dramatic Works*, pp. 210–12.

118 '*en finir avec cette autoenfoirade*': an allusion to Beckett's prose fragments *Pour finir encore et autre foirades*, the English title for *Foirades* being *Fizzles*, whose last, eighth fragment is titled 'For to end yet again'. See n. 38 and also p. 25 above. – Trans.

119 '*boire la mer*': the French idiom *ce n'est pas la mer à boire* means 'it's no big deal'. – Trans.

120 See n. 86 above. – Trans.

121 See Derrida, 'Rams', trans. Thomas Dutoit and Philippe Romanski, in *Sovereignties in Question: The Poetics of*

Paul Celan, ed. Thomas Dutoit and Outi Pasanen (New York: Fordham University Press, 2006), *passim*. – Trans.

122 In this sequence where Cixous freely adapts from Beckett's play, *pas* is to be heard in 'boots' (Beckett's own translation) as well as in the various renderings used so far. – Trans.

123 Beckett, *Embers*, p. 257. – Trans.

124 Friedrich Nietzsche's 'I call myself the last philosopher, because I am the last man', quoted by Derrida in 'Of an Apocalyptic Tone Once Adopted in Philosophy', trans. John P. Leavey, Jr, in *Derrida and Negative Theology*, ed. Harold G. Coward and Toby Foshay (Albany, NY: State University of New York Press, 1992), p. 49. – Trans.

125 Beckett, *Embers*, in *The Complete Dramatic Works*, p. 253 (translation slightly amended to reflect the French which Cixous discusses in the next paragraph).

126 This is a condensed reference to Stephen Dedalus's use of Shakespeare's life and works in the chapter 'Scylla and Charybdis' in Joyce's *Ulysses* in order to abolish his filial status and become his own father. – Trans.

127 Franz Kafka's imaginary 'dialogue' with his father Hermann in this autobiographical fiction *Letter to the Father* (*Brief an den Vater*). – Trans.

128 The other possible meaning of *facteur*: postman, with the undertones of the one who, like psychoanalysis, delivers the truthful letters of the unconscious – see Derrida's 'Le facteur de la vérité', in *The Post Card: From Socrates to Freud and Beyond*, trans., intro. and additional notes by Alan Bass (Chicago and London: University of Chicago Press, 1987), pp. 411–96 – is lost here, hence the bracketing off of 'f' to suggest some ambiguity in the original. – Trans.

129 In English in the text. – Trans.

130 In a discarded, short film called *The Professor*, Charlie Chaplin plays the trainer in a flea circus. After many failed attempts at reusing this six-minute sketch, it is said to have provided the inspiration for Chaplin's later film *Limelight*. – Trans.

131 Franz Kafka's parable *Before the Law*, the only part of his novel *The Trial* to be published in his lifetime, featuring a man from the country called Josef K. who wishes to gain entry to the law through a doorway and is told repeatedly that he cannot go through at the present time. – Trans.

132 See Beckett, *Cascando*, in *The Complete Dramatic Works*, *passim*. [In Greek mythology Sisyphus was cursed to keep rolling a huge boulder up a hill, only to watch it roll back down, an unending, repetitive, pointless chore which illustrates the 'action' of Beckett's short play. – Trans.]

133 The allusion here is to the French saying *en avoir l'air mais pas la chanson*, lit.: to have the tune (also, to look like it – hence the adaptive visual/aural play on 'too(n)' and 'tune' in the translation) but not the song, i.e. to have deceptive appearances. – Trans.

134 This paragraph works on the French pun *comment c'est*, *commencer*, left untranslated by Beckett himself (see p. 19 above). – Trans.

135 Beckett, *How It Is*, trans. from the French by the author (London: John Calder, 1964), pp. 105–7.

136 William Shakespeare, *Henry V*, Act III, Prologue, ll. 3–7; Act IV, Prologue, ll. 1–9.

137 Stephen Dedalus's famous description of the artist as omniscient God in James Joyce's *A Portrait of the Artist as a Young Man*, ed. Seamus Deane (Harmondsworth: Penguin, 1992), p. 233. – Trans.

138 Jacques Derrida, 'Psychoanalysis Searches the States of Its Soul: The Impossible Beyond of a Sovereign Cruelty', in *Without Alibi*, ed. and trans. Peggy Kamuf (Stanford: Stanford University Press, 2002), p. 255.

139 Derrida's notion of *déliaison*, introduced in several texts of the 1990s, which in deconstruction wishes to replace the bond or *socius* of any society or community, but here can also somehow be substituted for analysis (from *analuein*: to unbind). – Trans.

140 This well-known biblical parable has featured in several of Cixous's works of fiction, from the short story 'La Baleine de Jonas' (Jonah's Whale) onwards (in *Le Prénom de Dieu* [Paris: Grasset, 1967], pp. 165–83), and has been discussed by Jacques Derrida in *H. C. for Life, That Is to Say. . .*, trans., with additional notes, by Laurent Milesi and Stefan Herbrechter (Stanford: Stanford University Press, 2006), *passim*. – Trans.

141 References to the beginning of 'Imagination Dead Imagine', in *The Complete Short Prose*, p. 182. – Trans.

142 Beckett, 'The Calmative', trans. by the author, in *The Complete Short Prose*, p. 76.

143 In English in the text. Macbeth's final words in his famous tirade following the news of Lady Macbeth's death in Shakespeare's eponymous play, Act III, sc. v, l. 28. – Trans.